THE POWER OF READING

THE POWER OF READING

Insights from the Research

Stephen Krashen

1993
Libraries Unlimited, Inc.
Englewood, Colorado

LIBRARIES UNLIMITED, INC.
P.O. Box 6633
Englewood, CO 80155-6633
1-800-237-6124
www.lu.com

Library of Congress Cataloging-in-Publication Data

Krashen, Stephen D.
   The power of reading : insights from the research / Stephen
Krashen.
      x, 119 p. 17x25 cm.
      Includes bibliographical references and index.
      ISBN 1-56308-006-0
      I. Title.
Z1003.K917 1992
028'.9--dc20   92-15096
                                                    CIP

Contents

Contents

Acknowledgments

I thank David Loertscher and Suzanne Barchers for valuable suggestions, careful editing, and the margin notes. The author and publisher also thank the International Reading Association for permission to reprint table 2.2 and Ann Landers for permission to reprint a "letter to Ann Landers," which appears in Chapter 3 of this book.

Is There a Literacy Crisis?

I first heard about the literacy crisis in 1987 on the "Oprah Winfrey Show." Oprah Winfrey had as guests four adult "illiterates," people who, it was asserted, were completely unable to read and write. Their stories were touching and, by now, familiar to the reading public. They told how they had been "passed along" in school, surviving by paying careful attention in class and relying on friends. They had evolved strategies for getting through the day; for example, when they went to a restaurant with friends, they would wait to see what other people were ordering, then order the same thing.

Soon after this program, the plight of illiterates was dramatized in a made-for-TV movie starring Dennis Weaver. And soon after that, *Stanley and Iris* was released. Thanks to television shows such as "Oprah Winfrey," these films, and numerous articles in the press and in popular magazines, the public has the impression that a sizeable percentage of the public is completely illiterate, that the public schools are releasing hordes of young people who can't read. The public also has the impression that illiteracy is curable by tutoring sessions that teach nonreaders to read aloud—in other words, phonics.

Both impressions are wrong. There is no literacy crisis, at least not the kind of crisis the media has portrayed. There are, first of all, few total illiterates; there are few people who have been through our educational system who are completely unable to read and write. In fact, literacy, defined simply as the ability to read and write on a basic level, has been steadily rising in the United States for the last hundred years (see, e.g., Stedman and Kaestle 1987).

There is, however, a problem. Nearly everyone in the United States can read and write. They just don't read and write very well. Although basic literacy has been on the increase for the last century, the demands for literacy have been rising faster. Many people clearly don't read and write well enough to handle the complex literacy demands of modern society.

The cure for this kind of literacy crisis lies, in my opinion, in doing one activity, an activity that is all too often rare in the lives of many people: reading. Specifically, I am recommending a certain kind of reading—free voluntary reading (henceforth FVR). FVR means reading because you want to. For school-age children, FVR means no book report, no questions at the end of the chapter, and no looking up every vocabulary word. FVR means putting down a book you don't like and choosing another one instead. It is the kind of reading highly literate people do obsessively all the time.

I will not claim that FVR is the complete answer. Free readers are not all guaranteed admission to Harvard Law School. What the research tells me is that if children or less literate adults start reading for pleasure, however, good things will happen. Their reading comprehension will improve, and they will find difficult, academic-style texts more comprehensible. Their writing style will improve, and they will be better able to write prose in a style that is acceptable to schools, business, and the scientific community. Their vocabulary will improve and will improve at a better rate than if they took one of the well-advertised vocabulary building courses. Also, their spelling and control of grammar will improve.

In other words, free readers have a chance. The research also tells me, however, that those who do not develop the pleasure reading habit simply don't have a chance—they will have a very difficult time reading and writing at a level high enough to deal with the demands of today's world.

FVR is also, I am convinced, the way to achieve advanced second language proficiency. Although the research in second language reading is not as extensive as in first language reading, it strongly suggests that free reading in a second or foreign language is one of the best things an acquirer can do to bridge the gap from the beginning level to truly advanced levels of second language proficiency.

This book examines the research into FVR, the ways FVR may be implemented, and issues related to reading, writing, and literacy. The possibilities free voluntary reading offers individuals and society are great. The goal of this book is to show the reader what free voluntary reading has to offer.

The Research

Research studies of the nineteenth and twentieth centuries have explored the power of free voluntary reading to increase literacy. This chapter addresses the following questions:

1. *What is free voluntary reading?*
2. *How does FVR affect reading comprehension, spelling, vocabulary, grammar, and writing style?*
3. *What are the effects of FVR on second language acquisition?*
4. *How does FVR compare to traditional direct instruction?*

Free voluntary reading (henceforth FVR) is one of the most powerful tools we have in language education, and, as I argue in this chapter, FVR is the missing ingredient in first language "language arts" as well as in intermediate second and foreign language instruction. It will not, by itself, produce the highest levels of competence; rather, it provides a foundation so that higher levels of proficiency may be reached. When FVR is missing, these advanced levels are extremely difficult to attain.

☐ *Free voluntary reading (FVR) is the foundation of language education.*

In the following section, the evidence for the efficacy of FVR is briefly reviewed. Following this review, I argue that alternative means of promoting language and literacy development are not nearly as effective.

The Evidence

In-School Free Reading Programs

In-school free reading programs provide some of the clearest evidence for the power of reading. In these programs, part of the school day is set aside for unrestricted FVR. There are two kinds of in-school free reading programs: sustained silent reading and self-selected reading. In sustained silent reading, both students and teachers simply engage in free reading for short periods each day (from five to 15 minutes). In self-selected reading, free reading is a large part of the language arts program, with teachers holding regular conferences with students to discuss what was read.

□ *Sustained silent reading and self-selected reading are powerful tools.*

Table 1.1
Results of Reading Comprehension Tests of Students in In-School Free Reading Programs Compared to Students in Traditional Reading Instruction[1]

□ *In 38 of 41 studies, students using FVR did as well or better in reading comprehension tests than students given traditional skill-based reading instruction.*

Duration	Positive	Results[a] No Difference	Negative
Less than 7 months	5	13	3
7 months–1 year	3	8	0
Greater than 1 year	8	1	0

a. Includes sustained silent reading and self-selected reading programs.

Table 1.1 summarizes the impact of in-school free reading programs on standardized tests of reading comprehension. In each case, readers were compared to students participating in traditional language arts programs, programs that emphasize reading from the assigned basal reader and direct instruction in grammar, vocabulary, reading comprehension, and spelling.

Two findings clearly emerge from this table: First, in-school free reading programs are consistently effective. In 38 out of 41 comparisons (93 percent), readers do as well or better than students who were engaged in traditional language arts programs.

Note that a finding of "no difference" between free readers and students in traditional programs suggests that free reading alone is just as good as traditional instruction, which confirms that free reading results in literacy growth, an important theoretical point we return to later. Because free reading is so much more pleasant than regular instruction (for both students and teachers), this finding also provides evidence in favor of the use of free reading in classrooms.[2]

Second, studies that last longer show more consistently positive results. At least one reason for this finding is apparent to teachers who have used free reading in their classrooms: It takes a while for students to select a book. Table 1.1 suggests that programs that last for longer than a year are consistently effective.

□ *The longer FVR is practiced, the more consistent the results.*

In-school free reading programs are also effective for vocabulary development, grammar test performance, writing, and oral/aural language ability (for reviews, see Krashen 1985a, 1989; Elley 1991). Only a few in-school reading studies have measured gains in spelling. Of these, some show no difference between free reading and traditional instruction in spelling (Pfau 1967; Elley 1991, for one of three groups), and in some the readers made better progress (Collins 1980; Elley 1991, for one group of three groups of students).

☐ *Other types of students benefit from FVR:*

• *reform school boys,*

• *students in England,*

• *students studying English as a second language in Fiji,*

Some examples illustrate these findings. Nearly all of the research summarized in table 1.1 was performed on first language acquirers in elementary school in the United States. The results of four studies show that free reading is very effective with other groups as well.

McNeil (in Fader 1976) examined the effects of a free reading program on reform school boys, ages 12–17. After two years, the readers were superior to a comparison group in reading comprehension, writing fluency, writing complexity, attitude toward school, and self-esteem.

Southgate, Arnold, and Johnson (1981) reported that classes of seven- to nine-year-olds in England that made the greatest progress in reading achievement in one school year were those in which teachers devoted more time to "uninterrupted private reading and to discussion of books" (p. 254). (The authors found a negative correlation between progress in reading achievement and the amount of time teachers spent listening to children read aloud. Interestingly, three-fourths of the children said they preferred to read silently, rather than read aloud to someone else.)

Elley and Mangubhai (1983) showed that free reading has a dramatic effect on second language acquirers. Their subjects, fourth- and fifth-grade students of English as a foreign language in the Fiji Islands, were divided into three groups for their 30-minute daily English class. One group had traditional audio-lingual method instruction, a second did only free reading, while a third did "shared book experience," a program originated by Don Holdaway in which books of interest were read to the class (from "big books") and discussed with the students. After two years, the students in the free reading group and the shared book experience group were far superior to the traditional group in tests of reading comprehension, writing, and grammar.

Elley (1991) also showed that free reading had a profound effect on second language acquirers in Singapore. In three studies involving a total of approximately 3,000 children, ages six through nine, and lasting from one to three years, children who followed the "Reading and English Acquisition Program," a combination of shared book experience, language experience, and free reading ("book flood"), outperformed traditionally taught students on tests of reading comprehension, vocabulary, oral language, grammar, listening comprehension, and writing.

- *elementary-age children in Singapore.*

Reported Free Voluntary Reading

People who say they read more typically read better and have a more mature writing style. As is the case with in-school free reading, this result has been confirmed in many studies (for reviews, see Krashen 1985a, 1988). I present here only a few examples.

□ *People who say they read more write better.*

Anderson, Wilson, and Fielding (1988) asked fifth graders to record their activities outside of school and reported that "among all the ways children spent their time, reading books was the best predictor of several measures of reading achievement (reading comprehension, vocabulary, and reading speed), including gains in reading comprehension between second and fifth grade" (p. 285).

□ *Reading as a leisure activity is the best predictor of comprehension, vocabulary, and reading speed.*

The California Assessment Program (CAP; see Alexander 1986) reported a clear positive relationship

□ *Two studies reported higher scores on standardized tests when FVR was used.*

□ *However, skill-based reading exercises did not help comprehension levels.*

□ *Outstanding high school writers reported extensive summer reading.*

□ *College freshmen judged good writers dubbed themselves avid readers.*

between the amount eighth graders said they read per day and their scores on the CAP test of English and Language Arts. These tests cover reading comprehension, both "basic skills" and "critical thinking," as well as writing (punctuation, word choice, sentence style, paragraph development). Foertsch (1992) reported similar results: Fourth, eighth, and twelfth graders who reported more reading outside of school performed better on a test of reading comprehension. There was, however, no impact of traditional instruction on reading: Those who did more workbook assignments after reading did not read better, nor did those who had more instruction on the use of "reading skills" (e.g., prediction).

Applebee (1978) found that outstanding high school writers (winners of the National Council of Teachers of English achievement awards in writing) were pleasure readers. They reported reading an average of 14 books for pleasure over the summer vacation and an average of four books the first two months of their senior year. Comparison with other studies suggests that this is an extraordinary amount of reading; Brink (1939) reported that the high school students he studied read an average of three books during the summer; Gallo (1968) found that a group of eleventh graders averaged about 11 books per year.

In Kimberling, Wingate, Rosser, Dichara, and Krashen (reported in Krashen 1978, 1984), 66 college freshmen wrote essays at home, which were evaluated by two raters. Only essays judged to be "highly competent" and "of low competence" were retained in the study. Students were asked on a questionnaire to indicate how much reading they had done at different times in their lives. Very clear differences were found between good and poor writers: Good writers reported more pleasure reading at all ages, and especially during the high school years. In fact, not one poor writer reported "a lot" of pleasure reading during high school.

□ *Not one poor reader reported "a lot" of pleasure reading.*

Several studies confirm that those who read more in their second language also write better in that language (Salyer 1987; Janopoulos 1986; Kaplan and Palhinda 1981) and studies also show a relationship between measures of amount read and spelling performance (for first language acquisition, Stanovich and West 1989; for second language acquisition, Polak and Krashen 1988).

□ *Those who read in a second language write and spell better in that language.*

The relationship between reported free voluntary reading and literacy development is not always large, but it is remarkably consistent. Nearly every study that has examined this relationship has found a correlation, and it is present even when different tests, different methods of probing reading habits, and different definitions of free reading are used.

□ *The relationship between reported FVR and literacy is remarkably consistent.*

Although the results of reported free voluntary reading studies are impressive, there are some problems with this research. First, they rely on how much reading people say they do, which may or may not be accurate. Second, one can imagine other factors that could have been responsible for literacy development; perhaps those who read more also did other things, such as vocabulary exercises, or perhaps those who did more drills and exercises in school became better readers and thus read more. I think these possibilities are far-fetched, but they are possible. One could also argue that the in-school free reading studies discussed earlier also have this problem—maybe the additional reading inspired students to do more drills and exercises. This is also unlikely, but

□ *Other explanations for literacy development are possible but not plausible.*

possible. Such alternative explanations are, however, impossible for read and test studies, discussed in the next section.

Read and Test Studies

□ *Read and test studies utilize passages with unfamiliar words in context.*

In read and test studies, subjects read passages containing words whose meanings and spellings are unfamiliar to them. Readers are not alerted to the presence of these words in the text, nor are they told that a vocabulary or spelling test will be given after they read the text. Rather, readers are encouraged to read the passage for its meaning. After they finish reading the passage, they are tested to see if they have acquired some or all of the meaning of the unfamiliar words or if their spelling of these words has improved. Read and test studies thus probe "incidental" learning.

Some of the most important read and test studies were conducted at the University of Illinois (Nagy, Herman, and Anderson 1985; Nagy, Anderson, and Herman 1987). The Illinois researchers used elementary school students as subjects and passages from school textbooks as texts. Their measures of vocabulary knowledge had an important feature: They were sensitive to whether subjects had acquired just part of the meaning of a target word.

□ *Each time an unfamiliar word is seen in print, a small increase in word knowledge typically occurs.*

Nagy and colleagues (1985) concluded from their data that when an unfamiliar word was seen in print, "a small but statistically reliable increase of word knowledge" typically occurred (Nagy and Herman 1987, p. 26). They found that the chance of a reader acquiring a word from one exposure was between 5 and 20 percent, depending on the testing method used. This may not seem like very much, but the Illinois team argues that when we consider the amount of reading children do, even this small effect results in a great deal of vocabulary growth. They estimate that if children read about 1 million words per year, just a 5 percent chance of acquiring a word's meaning from context with each exposure will result in vocabulary growth of about 1,000 words per year, "well enough to pass fairly discriminating multiple-choice tests" (Nagy, Anderson, and Herman 1987, p. 262).

☐ *If children read 1 million words in a year, at least 1,000 words will be added to their vocabulary.*

One million words per year is an average dose of reading for middle-class children (Anderson, Wilson, and Fielding 1988) and is not too difficult to attain, if interesting reading material is available. Comic books, for example, contain at least 2,000 words, while teen romances, such as the Sweet Valley High series, contain 40,000 to 50,000 words (Parrish and Atwood 1985).

☐ *Reading 1 million words in a year is easily attainable by children.*

Of course, there is a great deal of variation around the 5–20 percent figure that Nagy and colleagues arrived at. Some contexts give the reader clearer clues to the meaning of a word than others do. Nevertheless, research indicates that most contexts are helpful; Beck, McKeown, and McCaslin (1983) found that 61 percent of the contexts they examined in basal readers were of help in acquiring new vocabulary, providing at least some clues to meanings of unfamiliar words, while 31 percent were of no help and 8 percent were "misdirective."

Despite the presence of occasionally unhelpful or misdirective contexts, readers eventually arrive at meanings of unknown words. The few that escape readers, that must be looked up or that readers get completely wrong, are a tiny minority compared to the enormous number successfully acquired.[3]

□ *Building a vocabulary through context is a gradual process.*

The research thus suggests that words are not learned all at once when they are seen in context. Rather, word knowledge grows in "small increments." At any given time, there are words we know well, words we do not know, and words in between—to increase our vocabulary, we need to follow Twadell's advice and learn to tolerate some vagueness, vagueness that is reduced bit by bit as we read more and encounter unfamiliar words more. At any given moment, Twadell notes, "we may 'know' a very large number of words with various degrees of vagueness—words which are in a twilight zone between the darkness of entire unfamiliarity and the brightness of complete familiarity" (Twadell 1973, p. 73).

The Clockwork Orange Study

The Clockwork Orange study (Saragi, Nation, and Meister 1978) provides a powerful demonstration of our ability to acquire vocabulary by reading. In this study, adult readers were asked to read *A Clockwork Orange* by Anthony Burgess, a novel that contains 241 words from a slang called *nadsat*. Each *nadsat* word is repeated an average of 15 times. Few readers know these words before reading the book. The versions of *A Clockwork Orange* sold in bookstores have a dictionary in the back, so readers can look up the meanings of the *nadsat* words.

□ *Students who read a novel with many unique words actually learned the meaning of many of those words from context clues only.*

In this study, subjects were simply asked to read *A Clockwork Orange* and were told that after they finished it, they would be given a test of comprehension and literary criticism. They were not told to try and learn or remember the *nadsat* words. What is crucial is that they were given copies of the book without the dictionary in the back. The subjects read the book on their own time and reported finishing it in three days or less. A few days later, subjects were given a multiple-choice test covering 90 of the *nadsat* words.

A great deal of vocabulary acquisition took place. Scores ranged from 50 percent to 96 percent correct, with an average of 76 percent—subjects picked up at least 45 words, simply by reading a novel.[4]

Spelling

Spelling read and test studies yield similar results (see Krashen 1989, for a detailed review). Each time readers read a passage containing words they cannot spell, they make a small amount of progress in acquiring the correct spelling.

□ *Spelling is also improved when reading is done.*

Nisbet's study (Nisbet 1941) is typical. Children ages 11 to 14 read passages containing words they could not spell correctly on a pretest. After reading the passage, they could spell an average of about one out of 25 of these words. Nisbet found this figure unimpressive and concluded that "intensive reading and study of a passage . . . does lead to some learning of spelling, but this gain is not sufficient . . . to justify the neglect of specific spelling instruction" (p. 11). As we just saw, however, Nagy, Herman, and Anderson (1985) found that vocabulary acquisition from reading occurs with similar efficiency. Thus, one out of 25 might be enough, if readers read enough.[5]

The hypothesis that spelling comes from reading is confirmed by an experience familiar to all teachers: Our spelling gets worse when we read misspelled words. A recent modified read and test study, in fact, confirmed that "reading student

☐ *If students read misspelled words, their spelling ability declines as does the confidence of the speller.*

essays may be hazardous to one's spelling accuracy" (Jacoby and Hollingshead 1990, p. 357). In this study, subjects read misspelled versions of frequently misspelled words, and correctly spelled versions of different words. Even though they read the misspelled words only once, when given a spelling test, the subjects performed significantly worse on the words they had seen misspelled than on those they had seen spelled correctly.

Jacoby and Hollingshead (1990) point out that the effect of seeing an incorrectly misspelled word just one time on spelling performance was not large. They noted, however, that

> much more dramatic results were produced . . . by the second author of [the] paper. In the course of collecting the data . . . she read the incorrectly spelled words a large number of times. As a result of this extended experience with those incorrect spellings, she reports having lost confidence in her spelling accuracy. She can no longer judge spelling accuracy on the basis of a word "looking right." The word might look right because it was one of our incorrectly spelled words . . . (pp. 356–357).

Summary

☐ *FVR results in better*
- *reading comprehension*
- *writing style*
- *vocabulary*
- *spelling*
- *grammatical development*

In-school free reading studies and "out of school" self-reported free voluntary reading studies show that more reading results in better reading comprehension, writing style, vocabulary, spelling, and grammatical development. Read and test studies confirm that reading develops vocabulary and spelling.[6] Figure 1.1 summarizes "the reading hypothesis."

Despite these results, it could be argued that reading is only one way to develop literacy. In the

Figure 1.1 The Reading Hypothesis

following section, we examine one rival hypothesis, the hypothesis that literacy can be developed in another way: by direct instruction.

The Alternative to Free Reading: Direct Instruction

Direct instruction can be characterized as a combination of two processes:

1. Skill-building: Skill-building means learning a rule, word meaning, or spelling consciously and then making the rule "automatic" through output practice.

☐ *Can direct (skill-based) reading instruction compete with FVR as the best method of improving literacy?*

2. Error correction: When errors are corrected, students are expected to adjust their conscious knowledge of the rule, word, or spelling.

There are several compelling reasons why direct instruction cannot account for the development of literacy. Each of these reasons, taken alone, is sufficient. Together, the case against instruction is overwhelming. Briefly, there are three arguments against instruction: 1) Language is too vast, too complex to be taught or learned one rule or word at a time (the complexity argument); 2) Literacy development can occur without formal instruction (competence without instruction);

☐ *The case against direct reading instruction is overwhelming.*

3) The impact of direct instruction is typically small or nonexistent. When studies do show an effect of instruction, the effect sometimes disappears with time.

The Complexity Argument

Many scholars have noted that language is too complex to be deliberately and consciously learned one rule or one item at a time. This argument has been made for the acquisition of grammar (Krashen 1982), spelling (Smith 1982a), phonics (Smith 1988a), writing style (Smith 1983; Krashen 1984), and vocabulary (Smith 1988a; Nagy, Herman, and Anderson 1985).

Perhaps the most concrete example is vocabulary. Estimates of adult vocabulary size range from about 40,000 (Lorge and Chall 1963) to 156,000 words (Seashore and Eckerson 1940), and it has been claimed that elementary school children acquire from eight (Nagy and Herman 1987) to more than 14 (Miller 1977) words per day.[7]

□ *Language is too complex to be learned one rule at a time.*

Not only are there many words to acquire, there are also subtle and complex properties of words that competent language users have acquired. Quite often, the meaning of a word is not nearly adequately represented by a synonym. As Finegan and Besnier (1989) point out, words that appear to have the same meaning often refer to slightly different concepts or are used in slightly different ways, and can have different social meanings.[8]

□ *Language users must acquire many words with many nuances of meaning and complex grammatical properties.*

Also, when we acquire a word we acquire considerable knowledge about its grammatical properties. With verbs, for example, this includes knowing whether they are transitive or intransitive, what kinds of complements they can be used with, and so on. Very little of this knowledge is deliberately taught.

Vocabulary teaching methods typically focus on teaching simple synonyms, and thus give only part of the meaning of the word, and none of its social meanings or grammatical properties. Intensive methods that aim to give students a thorough knowledge of words are not nearly as efficient as reading in terms of words gained per minute. In fact, Nagy, Herman, and Anderson (1985) argue that picking up word meanings by reading is 10 times faster than intensive vocabulary instruction. Their suggestion is not to do both instruction and reading—the time is better spent in reading alone.

☐ *Teaching vocabulary lists is inefficient—the time is better spent reading alone.*

Competence Without Instruction

There is abundant evidence that literacy development can occur without formal instruction. Moreover, this evidence strongly suggests that reading is potent enough to do nearly the entire job alone.

The read and test studies reviewed earlier are among the most compelling cases of literacy development without instruction. Clearly, in these cases, acquisition of vocabulary and spelling occurred without skill-building or correction.

Similarly, students in in-school free reading programs (see "In-School Free Reading Programs" above) who made gains equal to or greater than children in traditional programs have demonstrated acquisition of literacy without instruction, as do reports of the success of "whole language" programs (Hagerty, Hiebert, and Owens 1989; and Klesius, Griffith, and Zielonka 1991).

□ *Only a small percentage of people with large vocabularies and good writing ability used vocabulary books to increase their vocabularies.*

People with large vocabularies and good writing ability do not claim to have developed them through study. Smith and Supanich (1984) tested 456 company presidents and reported that they had significantly larger vocabulary scores than a comparison group of adults did. When asked if they had made an effort to increase their vocabulary since leaving school, 54.5 percent said they had. When asked what they did to increase their vocabulary, however, about half of the 54.5 percent mentioned reading. Only 14 percent of those who tried to increase their vocabulary (3 percent of the total group) mentioned the use of vocabulary books.

Some Case Histories

Some impressive case histories strongly suggest that reading alone is enough. Richard Wright (Wright 1966) grew up in an environment where reading and writing was disapproved of by family members; his grandmother actually burned the books he brought home, "branding them as worldly" (Wright 1966, p. 142).

Wright became interested in reading and in hearing stories at an early age, thanks to a schoolteacher (a boarder at his home) who told him stories from novels. Wright struggled to gain access to reading material. He delivered newspapers only so that he could read them and used an associate's library card to take books out of a library that was restricted to whites.

□ *Case in point: Author Richard Wright attributed his language development to novels, not English grammars.*

Clearly in agreement with the research reported here, Wright credits reading with providing his language development: "I wanted to write and I did not even know the English language. I bought English grammars and found them dull. I felt that

I was getting a better sense of the language from novels than from grammars" (p. 275).

Although Richard Wright depended, to a great extent, on fiction, Malcolm X (El-Hajj Malik El-Shabazz) credited nonfiction with his literacy development. As he describes in his autobiography, Malcolm X had early success in school. He was, in fact, president of his seventh-grade class. His life in the streets, however, "erased everything I'd ever learned in school" (El-Shabazz 1964, p. 154). As a prisoner, in his early twenties, his literacy level was low. He describes his first attempt to write a letter to Elijah Mohammed:

> At least twenty-five times I must have written that first one-page letter to him, over and over. I was trying to make it legible and understandable. I practically couldn't read my handwriting myself; it shames even to remember it. My spelling and grammar were as bad, if not worse (p. 169).

The change came in prison: "Many who hear me today somewhere in person, or on television, or those who read something I've said, will think I went to school far beyond the eighth grade. This impression is due entirely to my prison studies" (p. 171).

☐ *Malcolm X educated himself in prison by reading.*

These "prison studies" consisted largely of reading. Building his vocabulary at first the hard way, by studying the dictionary, Malcolm X became a dedicated reader: "In every free moment I had, if I was not reading in the library, I was reading on my bunk. You couldn't have gotten me out of books with a wedge . . ." (p. 173).

Like Richard Wright, Malcolm X specifically gave reading the credit: "Not long ago, an English writer telephoned me from London, asking questions. One was, 'What's your alma mater?' I told him, 'Books' " (p. 179).

These case histories are not hard data. Stories like these, however, are not uncommon, and it is difficult to imagine other sources for the literacy development that took place.

Spelling Without Instruction

There is excellent evidence that children can learn to spell without instruction. The earliest study showing this was by Cornman (1902), who studied the effect of dropping all spelling instruction in elementary schools for three years (spelling errors were still corrected by teachers, however). Cornman concluded that the effects of spelling instruction were "negligible" and that uninstructed students continued to improve in spelling and did just as well as students in previous years' classes and students in other schools.[9]

□ *Several studies show that children can learn to spell without instruction.*

Cornman's results were replicated by Richards (1920), who studied 78 children in grades 6, 7, and 8 who went without spelling instruction for one year. Richards reported that 67.5 percent of these children improved more than one year in spelling, 20.4 percent made no change, and only 12 percent got worse. An additional replication was done by Kyte (1948), who found that "excellent spellers" who were excused from spelling instruction continued to improve.

Preschoolers can learn to spell without instruction. Goodman and Goodman (1982) reported that their daughter Kay learned to read and spell before she came to school, without any formal instruction at home. At age six, Kay spelled 58 percent of the words on a third-grade spelling list correctly and

18

recognized the correct spellings of 91 percent of the words.

Several researchers have found that children can spell correctly a substantial percentage of words that they have not yet studied in class (Thompson 1930; Curtiss and Dolch 1939; Hughes 1966) and that children improve each year on words they already studied (Curtiss and Dolch 1939), which is additional evidence that spelling improves without instruction.

A recent study suggesting that adult second language acquirers can improve their spelling without instruction was done by Haggan (1991), who reported that fourth-year Arabic-speaking English majors at the University of Kuwait made fewer spelling errors in their writing than first-year English majors, even though little emphasis was put on "systematic, explicit teaching of spelling" (p. 59) in the curriculum.

□ *Adults learning English improve their spelling without instruction.*

The Effect of Instruction

The studies reviewed in "In-School Free Reading Programs" above show that when free reading and direct, or traditional, instruction are compared directly in method comparison studies, free reading nearly always proves to be superior on tests of reading comprehension, vocabulary, writing, and grammar. Recall that Foertsch (1992) found that more reading, whether self-selected or assigned (see note 6), was associated with better performance on a test of reading comprehension, but more workbook exercises were not. Recall also Nagy, Herman, and Anderson's conclusion, based on their read and test research (Nagy, Herman, and Anderson 1985), that picking up word meanings by reading is much more efficient than intensive

□ *FVR is nearly always superior to direct instruction on tests of:*
  - *reading comprehension*
  - *vocabulary*
  - *writing*
  - *grammar*

vocabulary instruction. In addition, Snow, Barnes, Chandler, Goodman, and Hemphill (1991) reported no significant correlations between the amount of explicit vocabulary instruction students had and gains in reading comprehension and vocabulary over four years. Snow et al. also found that the exclusive use of a basal reader or workbook in reading lessons was negatively correlated with vocabulary growth, but that the use of a workbook for homework was positively correlated with gains in reading comprehension, a result that conflicts with Foertsch's findings as well as other results presented in this section.

Although the research on the impact of in-school free reading on spelling was not conclusive, there is, however, extensive evidence from other sources showing that instruction has little effect on spelling. Rice (1897) claimed to find no correlation between the amount of time children were instructed in spelling and their spelling performance.[10] Additional evidence that spelling instruction is not very effective comes from Brandenberg (1919), who reported no improvement in spelling accuracy among college students after their psychology papers were "persistently and clearly" marked for spelling errors for one semester.

☐ *Almost all studies showed little improvement in spelling competence through direct instruction.*

Finally, Cook (1912) showed that students have a very hard time learning and applying spelling rules. Cook gave a total of 69 high school and college students a spelling test containing words that exemplified spelling rules the students had studied the previous semester. He found no difference in accuracy among students who said they knew the rules and used them while spelling the test words, those who knew the rules but did not use them, and those who did not know the rules at

☐ *Learning spelling rules is of dubious value.*

all. Also, the college students did better on the test, but the high school students knew more spelling rules, confirming a lack of a relationship between knowing the rule and spelling accuracy.[11]

I have found only two studies in which spelling instruction had a clear effect. In Thompson (1930), instruction accounted for approximately a half-year extra growth over and above that expected without instruction. I have pointed out, however (Krashen 1989), that Thompson's students put in a huge amount of time in spelling instruction. In Hamill, Larsen, and McNutt (1977), students who had spelling instruction were clearly ahead of uninstructed children in grades 3 and 4; this advantage, however, washed out by grades 5 and 6: At this level there was no difference between instructed and uninstructed children in spelling accuracy as measured by a standard spelling test. Spelling instruction, even when it works, may only succeed in helping children learn to spell words that they would have learned to spell on their own anyway.[12]

□ *When spelling instruction works, it may only be helping children learn to spell words they will learn to spell on their own from reading.*

Wilde (1990) estimated that each spelling word learned through direct instruction requires about 20 minutes of instructional time! Here is her logic: Spelling programs, she estimated, cover about 720 words per year and typically take up 15 minutes per day, or 45 hours per year. Children, however, have probably acquired about 65 percent of the words before the words are taught and acquire another 12 percent incidentally during the year, a total of 77 percent. Assuming they reach 95 percent mastery of the spelling list (an optimistic assumption), this means that instruction was responsible for 18 percent of the 720 words (95 percent minus 77 percent), or 130 words. At 45 hours per year, this means each word took about 20 minutes to learn to spell.

A series of studies, dating from 1935, confirm that grammar instruction has no impact on reading and writing (see reviews by Krashen 1984 and Hillocks 1986). The most recent and probably the most thorough is the New Zealand study (Elley, Barham, Lamb, and Wyllie 1976). High school students were divided into three groups: One group studied traditional grammar in English classes, a second studied transformational grammar, and a third studied no grammar. Students were tested every year for three years. Elley et al. found no differences in reading comprehension, writing style, writing mechanics, or vocabulary among the groups, and a follow-up done one year after the project ended also showed no differences among the groups. The authors concluded that "it is difficult to escape the conclusion that English grammar, whether traditional or transformational, has virtually no influence on the language growth of typical secondary students" (pp. 17–18).

□ *Teaching grammar has no influence on language growth of typical secondary students.*

Conclusion

In face-to-face comparisons, reading is consistently shown to be more efficient than direct instruction. Other studies confirm that direct instruction has little or no effect. The only conclusion we can draw from these findings can be stated easily: Reading is a powerful means of developing literacy, of developing reading comprehension ability, writing style, vocabulary, grammar, and spelling. Direct instruction is not.

An Interpretation

Studies showing that reading enhances literacy development lead to an uncontroversial conclusion: Reading is good for you. The research supports a stronger conclusion, however: Reading is the only way, the only way we become good readers, develop a good writing style, an adequate vocabulary, advanced grammar, and the only way we become good spellers.

□ *Reading may be the only way to develop literacy skills.*

There are two reasons for suspecting that this stronger conclusion is correct. First, the major alternative to reading, direct instruction, is not of much help. Second, research and theory in other areas come to the same conclusion. Reading researchers have concluded that we "learn to read by reading," that we learn to read by attempting to make sense of what we see on the page (Goodman 1982; Smith 1988a). In my work in language acquisition, I have concluded that we acquire language in only one way: by understanding messages, or obtaining "comprehensible input" in a low-anxiety situation (e.g., Krashen 1982, 1985b). This is precisely what free voluntary reading is: messages we understand presented in a low-anxiety situation.

□ *The research is consistent with theories of reading development and language acquisition.*

If this conclusion is true, if reading is the only way, it means we have to reconsider and reanalyze what we are doing when we attempt to teach language directly, with drills and exercises: All we are doing when we teach language this way is testing. Traditional language arts instruction, in other words, is merely a test, a test that privileged children, who grow up with books, pass and that less fortunate children fail.

□ *Direct language instruction with drills and exercises is merely testing.*

Let me make this very concrete. Every Monday, in thousands of language and language arts classes, children are given a list of 20 vocabulary words. During the week they do "skill-building" exercises: Draw a line from the word to the definition, fill-in-the-blank, write three sentences with each word. On Friday, the children are tested on the words.

☐ *Readers pass vocabulary tests. Nonreaders struggle.*

If you show the list of 20 words to a child who has read, who grew up with books, he probably knows 15 or 16 of the words already. He has seen them before, in *Choose Your Own Adventure*, in *Spider-Man*, and in *The Dungeon Master's Handbook*. If he studies, he gets an A. If he does not study, he gets a B.

If you show the list of 20 words to a child who did not grow up with books, the situation is very different. He may know five or six of the words. If he studies, with a heroic effort, he might get a D+. Direct language instruction for these children may be nothing more than a test that they fail. And like victims of child abuse, they blame themselves.[13]

☐ *More drills for poor readers do not work.*

What do we typically do for children who did not grow up with books? More drills and exercises, more of what does not work. The title of Allington's 1980 paper summarizes the results of his research: "Poor readers don't get to read much in reading groups." Those who can read well are allowed to do more free reading. Those behind in reading have to do more work sheets, workbook pages, and exercises, a practice that can only increase the gap.

The Schoolboys of Barbiana, a group of eight teenagers who were unable to succeed in the Italian school system (Schoolboys of Barbiana 1970), understood that school is a test. Their thorough analysis of failure in Italian schools revealed an undeniable social class bias: At every level, children of the poor failed at higher rates than children of professional classes. The parents of those who fail, according to the Schoolboys, are persuaded to blame the children:

> The poorest among the parents . . . don't even suspect what is going on. . . . If things are not going so well, it must be that their child is not cut out for studying. "Even the teacher said so. A real gentleman. He asked me to sit down. He showed me the record book. And a test all covered with red marks. I guess we just weren't blessed with an intelligent boy. He will go to work in the fields, like us" (p. 27).

The Schoolboys, however, placed the reason for the failure of these children elsewhere. One reason they gave is that those who are successful come to school already literate.

Teachers in intermediate schools (grades 6–8) feel they are teaching literacy, because they see improvement: "When they came into the first intermediate [grade 6], they were truly illiterate. But now, all their papers are all correct." What has really happened is that the less literate students have failed and have left school:

☐ *The less literate are the first to fail and drop out of school.*

> Who is she talking about? Where are the boys she received in the first? The only ones left are those who could write correctly to begin with; they could probably write just as well in the third elementary. The ones who learned to write at home.
>
> The illiterate she had in the first grade are just as illiterate now. She has simply dropped them from sight (p. 49).

The problem, the Schoolboys conclude, needs to be solved at school:

☐ *Using traditional methods in school is like having a hospital that tends to the healthy and rejects the sick.*

At times the temptation to get rid of them (children of the poor) is strong. But if we lose them, school is no longer school. It is a hospital which tends to the healthy and rejects the sick. It becomes just a place to strengthen the existing differences to a point of no return (pp. 12–13).

Notes

☐ *Note 1 documents the research studies summarized in table 1.1.*

1. The following studies were used to compile table 1.1:

Duration less than 7 months

Positive: Wolf and Mikulecky 1978; Aranha 1985; Gordon and Clark 1961; Holt and O'Tuel 1989 (grade 7); Husar 1967 (grade 6).

No Difference: Sperzl 1948; Oliver 1973; Oliver 1976; Evans and Towner 1975; Collins 1980; Schon, Hopkins, and Vojir 1984 (Tempe); Sartain 1960 ("good readers" group); Holt and O'Tuel 1989 (grade 8); Summers and McClelland 1982 (3 groups); Husar 1967 (grades 4, 5).

Negative: Lawson 1968; Sartain 1960 ("slow readers" group); San Diego County 1965.

Duration 7 months to one year

Positive: Elley 1991 (Singapore, P1 survey); Jenkins 1957; Bader, Veatch, and Eldridge 1987.

No Difference: Schon, Hopkins, and Vojir 1985 (Chandler); Schon, Hopkins, and Vojir 1985 (grade 7); Schon, Hopkins, and Vojir 1985 (grade 8); McDonald, Harris, and Mann 1966; Greaney 1970; Davis and Lucas 1971 (grades 7, 8); Healy 1963.

Duration longer than one year

Positive: Elley and Mangubhai 1983 (grades 4, 5); Elley 1991 (Singapore, sample of 512); Elley

1991 (Singapore, P3 survey); Aronow 1961; Bohn-horst and Sellars 1959; Cyrog 1962; Johnson 1965.

No Difference: Elley et al. 1976.

2. In all the studies used in table 1.1, free reading was included as part of regular instruction, that is, it was not supplementary. The following table presents free reading studies in which free reading was not a part of regular language arts instruction but was added on.

☐ *Note 2 analyzes studies where FVR was added to the regular language arts program.*

Duration	Positive	Results No Difference	Negative
Less than 7 months	4	0	0
7 months–1 year	1	3	0
Greater than 1 year	0	1	0

Although there are no negative results, "no difference" in this case (as contrasted to table 1.1 in the text) is a cause for concern, because free reading did not replace traditional instruction. In one of the four "no difference" cases, however, there is a clear explanation for these results: In Maynes (1981), children were scheduled for free reading during their lunch period(!). Also, in Pfau (1967), no additional gains were found for reading comprehension and spelling, but the readers did make superior gains in vocabulary and writing complexity. In Manning and Manning (1984), students who engaged in sustained silent reading made better gains than a comparison group, but the difference was not significant. Sustained silent reading was significantly better than traditional instruction, however, when readers interacted with each other, that is, when they discussed their reading with each other and shared books.

A comparison group was used in all studies included in table 1.1. Other studies did not use comparison groups but simply compared students to published norms, to expected growth. Although there are numerous problems with this approach (see, e.g., Campbell and Stanley 1966), the results of these studies are quite remarkable: Eighteen comparisons are in favor of free reading, with no studies showing "no difference" and only one negative result (see Krashen 1985a, 1988 for details).

3. Most of the contexts in Schatz and Baldwin (1986) were not helpful or "facilitative"; readers could not successfully acquire unfamiliar words from them. Passages used, however, were only three sentences long. Determining the meaning of some words may take more than three sentences. Consider this example from Schatz and Baldwin: "He takes out an envelope from a drawer, and takes paper money from it. He looks at it ruefully, and then with decision puts it into his pocket, with decision takes down his hat. Then dressed, with indecision looks out the window to the house of Mrs. Lithebe, and shakes his head" (p. 443).

From just the passage, it is very hard to arrive at the meaning of "ruefully." With wider context (the whole book) and a deeper understanding of the character and what has happened in the story, the reader would have a much better chance.

Some experimenters have been able to improve vocabulary acquisition by rewriting texts to make contexts more "facilitative" or "considerate." Although readers in these studies are able to acquire more vocabulary from altered texts, readers still acquire an impressive amount from the original, unaltered texts (Herman et al. 1987; Konopak 1988).

4. See Pitts, White, and Krashen (1989) for a successful partial replication of the Clockwork Orange study using second language acquirers.

5. See Ormrod (1986) for recent results similar to Nisbet's, and a similar interpretation. Gilbert's studies (Gilbert 1934a, 1934b, 1935) were, to my knowledge, the first read and test studies showing that spelling knowledge can be increased by reading.

6. What about assigned reading? It is reasonable to expect that assigned reading will have an impact on literacy development if it is interesting and comprehensible. The results of three studies support this conclusion. Harris (1949) found that teacher-selected books were effective for first graders. Her students did no drills or exercises and did not use a basal reader. Classwork included hearing stories read aloud and discussing the stories. After one year, the class median reading score was well above norms. Rehder (1980) reported spectacular gains in reading comprehension and vocabulary scores for high school students who completed a one-semester course on popular literature, which included required reading and a limited amount of self-selection (students were allowed to choose some of the reading from a list). Foertsch (1992) reported that more assigned textbook reading and more assigned reading of novels, poems, and stories were associated with better reading achievement. However, O'Brian (1931) reported that a traditional skill-building program was superior to an extensive reading program for fifth- and sixth-grade students. The reading, however, was assigned reading on social science topics, not selected by the students. Although there is, of course, good reason to assign certain books (see

☐ *Note 6 explores research where literature is used as the basis of reading instruction.*

Chapter 3, "Conclusions"), including self-selected reading is important because it ensures that reading is understandable and is for genuine interest. (For additional discussion of assigned reading, see Chapter 2, "Direct Encouragement.")

□ *Note 7 examines additional studies of adult vocabulary size.*

7. D'Anna, Zechmeister, and Hall (1991) have claimed that educated adults know only about 16,785 words. They had to work very hard to arrive at this figure, however. They eliminated hyphenated words (e.g., free-lance), capitalized words, foreign words, words "identified as old use" (e.g., forsooth), letters and names of letters (alpha), abbreviations, slang, and "multi-word entries" (e.g., video cassette). In fact, a perfect score on their test would have shown an estimated vocabulary size of fewer than 27,000 words, a figure considerably lower than previous conservative estimates of adult vocabulary size (e.g., Lorge and Chall 1963). Goulden, Nation, and Read (1990) arrived at a similar estimate employing similar means; their pool of potentially known words was 58,000.

8. Finegan and Besnier provide this example: "Even though *movie, film, flick* and *motion picture* all have the same referential meaning, the terms differ in social and affective meaning. *Film* strikes (North Americans) as a British word or a word that applies more to movie classics or art movies. *Flick* is recognized as a term that can be used only in the most informal contexts. The term *motion picture* is quaintly outdated; if someone were to use it in a conversation, it would be for its connotation as a term from the thirties or forties. Thus we can consider the terms synonymous if we specify that we are taking only referential meaning into consideration. At the social and affective levels, the terms are not synonymous" (1989, p. 184).

9. For a reanalysis of Cornman's data using modern statistical procedures, see Krashen and White (1991). We confirmed that Cornman's conclusions were basically correct; uninstructed students did just as well as instructed students on spelling words in their own compositions. We found some effect for formal instruction in spelling on some of the tests that focused students on form, that encouraged the use of conscious knowledge. This finding is consistent with current language acquisition theory (Krashen 1982).

□ *Notes 9 and 10 discuss reanalyses of older studies.*

10. See Krashen and White (1991) for a reanalysis of these data, which confirm Rice's claims. As in our reanalysis of Cornman (1902; see note 9, this chapter), spelling instruction had some effect on tests in which students were focused on form.

11. Cook also reported that even though the students had just studied the rules, many could not recall them. Of those who did recall rules, the version they gave was often much simpler than the version they were recently taught: "Curiously enough, most of the collegians who cited a version of the ie/ei rule as consciously used relied upon the word 'Alice' and other mnemonic devices which gave a clue to only one or two of the 11 words (relating to the ie/ei rule). . . . No [high school] freshman cited the rule as recently taught, but four had it almost correct. . . . Three [high school] seniors gave the rule substantially as taught, but nearly all the others who cited anything gave a version of something taught in earlier years, the 'Alice' rule, etc. The rule seems more likely to stick as first learned . . ." (Cook 1912, p. 322).

□ *Note 11 discusses learning rules of spelling.*

(The "Alice rule" is new to me; apparently it reminds writers that "i" comes before "e" except after "c.")

12. Note that Hammill, Larsen, and McNutt's results are also strong evidence that spelling development can occur without instruction, confirming the results of studies presented earlier.

☐ *Note 13 discusses the vast differences in children's vocabularies.*

13. Research confirms that the difference among children in vocabulary size is enormous. M. Smith (1941) found, in fact, that some first graders had larger vocabularies than some high school students. According to Smith, the range of basic words known by first graders was from 5,500 to 32,000, and for twelfth graders from 28,200 to 73,200. Other researchers have come up with more conservative data, but still conclude that there are huge differences among children. White, Graves, and Slater (1990) concluded that "mainstream" children know about 50 percent more words than "disadvantaged" children (see also Graves, Brunett, and Slater 1982).

What is clear is that some children have acquired much larger vocabularies than others. Nagy and Herman (1987) argue that "children who acquire a larger than average vocabulary—who could easily be learning 1,000 words per year over and above those learned by the average student—are not doing so simply through better vocabulary lessons" (p. 96), they are doing so by reading.

The Cure

2

If the full power of free voluntary reading is to be exploited, certain foundation elements must be in place over a long period of time. This chapter answers the following questions:
1. How does a print-rich environment affect FVR?
2. What is the role of public and school libraries?
3. How does reading aloud affect literacy?
4. Do direct encouragement and rewards increase reading?
5. What is the effect of light reading of comic books and teen romances?

If the arguments presented in the previous chapter are correct, if free voluntary reading is the only way to develop adequate levels of reading comprehension, writing style, vocabulary, grammar, and spelling, the implications are clear: One of our major goals in language education should be to encourage free reading, to make sure it happens. While we have paid lip-service to the value of reading (the shopping bag I got from the market recently proclaimed: "Make reading your bag: open books = open doors"), there has been only limited real effort in this direction.

□ *One of the major goals of language education should be to encourage free reading.*

Access

The most obvious step is to provide access to books. It is certainly true that "you can lead a horse to water but you cannot make him drink." But first we must make sure the water is there.

The research supports the commonsense view that when books are readily available, when the print environment is rich, more reading is done. A rich print environment in the home is related to how much children read; children who read more have more books at home (Morrow 1983; Neuman 1986; Greaney and Hegarty 1987).[1]

Enriching the print environments in classrooms has been shown to result in more reading. Morrow and Weinstein (1982) reported that installing well-designed library corners in kindergarten classes that previously did not have them resulted in more use of books and other "literature activities" by children during free play time. In addition, children did more free reading when the books in the library corner were more physically accessible, when they were within the children's reach, and when teachers allowed the children to take books home from the classroom library (Morrow 1982).

□ *Access to a school library results in more reading.*

Enriching the print environment by means of a school library results in more reading. Cleary (1939) reported that children in a school with no school library averaged 3.8 books read over a four-week period, while children from a school with a school library averaged exactly double, 7.6 books. Moreover, children from the school with the library read "better" books; 84 percent of the books they selected were on "approved" lists, compared to 65 percent of the reading done by the children with no library. Gaver (1963) reported that children who had access to school libraries did more reading than children who only had access to centralized book collections (without librarians), who in turn read more than children who only had access to classroom collections. My reanalysis of Gaver's data showed a strong correlation (r = .772) between the number of volumes available to the children and the amount they reported reading.

□ *Having a school librarian makes a difference in the amount read.*

Access to public libraries also affects how much children read: Heyns (1978) reported that children who live closer to public libraries read more. Snow, Barnes, Chandler, Goodman, and Hemphill (1991) did not distinguish between school and public libraries but found a significant positive correlation ($r = .39$) between number of library visits and gains over four years in reading comprehension (but not vocabulary, $r = .16$). Foertsch (1992) also did not distinguish between school and public libraries but reported that students who never took books out of libraries scored lower on a test of reading comprehension. Foertsch found, however, no clear relationship between frequency of library use and reading comprehension among library users.

☐ *Access to public libraries also affects how much children read.*

Access also influences library use. Students take more books out of school libraries that have more books and that stay open longer (Houle and Montmarquette 1984). Both of these factors apparently have dramatic effects; increasing the supply of books by 20 percent, according to Houle and Montmarquette, increases the number of books taken out by about 10 percent (for the statistically minded, the "elasticity" of number of books in the library was nearly .5), and increasing library hours about 20 percent increases loans by 17 percent in high school libraries and about 3.5 percent in elementary school libraries.

☐ *Larger school library collections and longer hours increase circulation.*

Figure 2.1 summarizes the relationship between the print environment, free voluntary reading, and the development of literacy. Confirmation that figure 2.1 is correct comes from studies of the effect of the print environment on literacy development directly, indicated by the dotted line in figure 2.1. These studies show consistent results.

Figure 2.1 The Relationship of Print Environment and Free Voluntary Reading to Literacy Development

□ *The richer the print environment, the better the literacy development.*

The richer the print environment, that is, the more reading material available, the better the literacy development. (Research reviewed in Krashen 1985a, 1988, 1989; Snow, Barnes, Chandler, Goodman, and Hemphill [1991] and Foertsch [1992] are recent confirmations of the association between print environment and literacy development.) Although the relationship between the richness of the print environment and literacy development is nearly always positive, the strength of the relationship found by researchers is often modest. One likely reason for this is that there is a missing link, or a "mediating variable": actual free reading, as illustrated in figure 2.1. A rich print environment will only result in more literacy development if more reading is done.

□ *However, a rich print environment helps only when more reading is done.*

Providing access to books is thus a necessary, but not sufficient, condition for encouraging reading. Other factors act to make free reading more desirable.

Comfort and Quiet

□ *A good reading environment encourages reading.*

The physical characteristics of the reading environment are important. Morrow (1983) reported that preschool and kindergarten children used the library corner more when it had pillows, easy chairs, and carpets, and when it was partitioned off and quiet.

A particularly fascinating result is reported by Greaney and Hegarty (1987), who found that parents of fifth graders classified as heavy readers allowed their children to read in bed more than parents of fifth graders classified as nonreaders. Of the heavy readers, 72.2 percent of their parents allowed reading in bed, compared to only 44.4 percent of the nonreaders' parents.

Libraries

My suspicion is that the first two conditions, access to books and comfort and quiet, are rarely met in many students' lives, in school or outside of school. One place where these conditions can be met is the library. If many students do indeed lack access to books and if the arguments for reading as the source of literacy development are even partly correct, libraries are crucially important.

☐ *Libraries are a consistent and major source of books for free reading.*

Children get a substantial percentage of their books from libraries. Table 2.1 combines data from several different studies in which elementary school students were asked where they got their books for free reading.

There is some variation in the data—in Lamme's study (1976), for example, the school library was the most popular, while in Ingham's outer city sample (1981), the classroom library was used more. There is good agreement in all studies, however, that children get much of their reading from some kind of library. Undoubtedly, ease of use, accessibility, and selection determine whether classroom, school, or public libraries are used more. In addition, 45 percent of the fifth graders questioned by Wendelin and Zinck (1983) reported that the library was the primary source of their reading, while the results of a study done in England

☐ *Children get much of their reading from libraries.*

reveal that 54.5 percent of adults get their books from public libraries (Luckman 1971, cited in Chandler 1973).

Table 2.1
Percentage of Books Children Obtain from Libraries
(Public, School, or Classroom) for Pleasure Reading

Study	7-9	Age 9	10	11	12	9-13
Lancaster, 1928						86
Cleary, 1939					66	
Gaver, 1963				30-63		
Lamme, 1976		89	84	81		
Ingham, 1978[a]			99	97	89	
Ingham, 1978[b]			88	72	84	
Swanton, 1984				70		
Southgate et al., 1981	50					

a. "outer city" schools
b. "inner city" schools

□ *Larger libraries are associated with better reading.*

□ *Larger school library collections mean higher reading scores.*

If libraries are a major source of books, and if more reading means better reading, larger libraries should be associated with better reading. This has been found to be the case for both first and second language acquisition. Gaver (1963) reported that children in schools with larger collections (full school libraries) made better gains in reading than did children in schools with smaller central collections, who in turn made better gains than children in schools that had only classroom collections. Elley and Mangubhai (1979; reported in Elley 1984) found that the most important predictor of English reading scores among children in the Fiji Islands was the size of the school library: "Those schools with libraries of more than 400 books produced consistently higher mean scores

than those with smaller libraries or none at all . . .
no school had high scores without a large library"
(p. 293).

Reading Aloud

Children who are read to at home read more
on their own (Lomax 1976; Neuman 1986), and
when teachers read stories to children and discuss
the stories ("literature activities"), children read
more (Morrow and Weinstein 1982, 1986). Research on the effects of in-school reading aloud to
children on increasing interest in reading has been
done at the kindergarten level (Morrow and Weinstein 1982) and grade 2 (Morrow and Weinstein
1986). The research then jumps to the college level:
In Pitts (1986), "basic skills" university students
("intelligent but underprepared students of all
ages entering college for the first time," p. 37) were
read to one hour per week for 13 weeks. Selections
included works by Twain, Salinger, Poe, and
Thurber, and the reading was discussed after-
wards. Pitts reported that the class that was read
to checked out more books, and better books, from
the reading lab than did students in other basic
skills classes. In addition, the class that was read
to did better on the final essay.

Reading aloud has, apparently, multiple effects
on literacy development. As noted above, it has an
indirect effect—hearing stories and discussing stories encourages reading, which in turn promotes
literacy development. There is a great deal of
evidence that hearing stories has a direct impact
on literacy development as well. In controlled
studies, it has been shown that children who are
read to regularly for several months make superior
gains in reading comprehension and vocabulary

☐ *Children read more when
they*
- *listen to stories*
- *discuss stories*

☐ *Even college students read
more and better books when
they are read to.*

☐ *Hearing stories has a direct
impact on literacy development.*

(Cohen 1968; Feitelson, Kita, and Goldstein 1986), and short-term studies show significant increases in vocabulary knowledge after just a few hearings of stories containing unfamiliar words (Eller, Pappas, and Brown 1988; Elley 1989; Leung and Pikulski 1990; Stahl, Richek, and Vandevier 1991).

Reading Experience

Reading itself promotes reading. A consistent finding in in-school free reading studies is that children who participate in these programs do more free reading than children in traditional comparison programs. Pfau (1967) is a good example: First graders participating in a sustained silent reading program for two years made more trips to the library, took out more books from the library, and mentioned reading more often when questioned about their leisure-time activities, when compared to children in traditional classes.

☐ *Three studies support the idea that reading itself promotes reading.*

Greaney and Clarke (1975) present spectacular results: Sixth-grade boys who participated in an in-school free reading program for eight and one-half months not only did more leisure reading while they were in the program, but also were still reading more than comparison students six years later.

Rucker (1982) provides one of the strongest demonstrations of the power of reading itself to stimulate interest in more reading. Rucker gave junior high school students questionnaires probing their interests. A few months later, he provided a random sample of the students with two free magazine subscriptions relating to their interests. One group of students received the magazine for a year, another for a year and a half. Neither the students, nor their teachers, nor their parents were informed that an experiment was being conducted, and even teachers did not know about the subscriptions.

Rucker reported that students who received the magazines had superior gains on standardized tests of reading (but not on tests of "language," e.g., mechanics and spelling, and math). A reasonable interpretation of these results is that the magazines themselves served as valuable input and that they stimulated even more reading. As Rucker points out, magazines are the most "reader interest specific" of all mass media and "may thus consequently be the most valuable as stimuli to reading" (p. 33).

☐ *Magazine reading appears to promote more reading.*

Do Rewards Work?

The studies discussed in the previous section suggest that the intrinsic reward of reading is so great that it will stimulate additional reading. We may not need extrinsic rewards for reading, that is, gold stars, cash awards, reading club memberships, or other incentives. Smith (1988b) argues, in fact, that rewards can backfire:

☐ *Extrinsic reading rewards may not be necessary and may backfire.*

> Show a child that the payoff for reading or writing something is a treat, a token, a happy face or a high mark, and that is what the child will learn is the price literacy should extract. Every child knows that anything accomplished by coercion, no matter how benign, cannot be worth doing in its own right (p. 124).

There are, however, cases in which extrinsic motivation did apparently work. Some of the subjects who wrote "reading autobiographies" in Carlsen and Sherrill (1988) reported that rewards got them started reading and kept them reading:

> Every fall the big event in my life from third through eighth grade was the awarding of book worm pins by the Public Library to those who had successfully read and reported on 15 books during the summer—so much that my mother always had a hard time getting me to help around the house (p. 14).

Rewards might serve, in some cases, as a jump-start; once the child starts reading, the intrinsic pleasure of reading takes over. Rewards do not always work, however. The following case suggests that Smith's analysis of the effects of rewards is correct.

> There are always summer inducements to make a child read. There were summer reading clubs with prizes for the highest quantity of books read and later, certificates and gold seals in the upper elementary school for reading and reporting on ten books a year. I always enrolled, because it was the socially acceptable thing to do. I never finished because books were for school, and running, jumping and playing was for fun (Carlsen and Sherrill [1988], p. 139).

Models

□ *Children read more when they see other people reading.*

Children read more when they see other people reading, both at school and at home. Morrow (1982) found that nursery school and kindergarten use of library corners increased when teachers read during sustained silent reading sessions. Morrow (1983) and Neuman (1986) reported that parents of children who do more leisure reading read more than parents of children who show less interest in books. Although these parents might do other things that promote reading, these results indicate that having a model is important.

These studies suggest that teachers should follow McCracken and McCracken's advice (McCracken and McCracken 1978) and actually read for pleasure themselves during sustained silent reading time. This may be difficult, given the endless paperwork teachers have to deal with, but the results will probably make the sacrifice worthwhile.

☐ *Teachers need to be models by reading for pleasure when students are reading.*

Direct Encouragement

Research is sparse in this area, but it appears that simply telling children to read may have an impact on the amount of reading done. Morrow (1982) reported that when nursery school and kindergarten teachers encouraged pupils to use the library corner more, the pupils did so. Lamme (1976) found that elementary school classroom libraries were used more when teachers "encouraged their use." Greaney and Hegarty (1987) found that 73 percent of the parents of "heavy readers" in the fifth grade encouraged their children to read specific books, as compared to 44 percent of the parents of nonreaders.

☐ *Direct encouragement to read helps if the right type of reading material is recommended.*

Conversely, directing children to read may backfire if the reading material is not appropriate. Greaney and Hegarty also reported that more parents of nonreaders encouraged newspaper reading (41 percent, compared to 18 percent of the parents of nonreaders). One interpretation of this result is that newspaper reading was not right for fifth graders.

The case of Ben Carson suggests that direct encouragement to read can stimulate an interest in reading, and thus lead to better literacy development. Carson, now a neurosurgeon, was a poor student in the fifth grade when his mother required him to check out two books per week from

☐ *The Ben Carson story of books and reading is a significant example.*

the library and insisted that he report on his reading to her at the end of each week. Carson was not enthusiastic but obeyed his mother. What is crucial is that Carson's mother allowed him to read whatever he wanted. At first, Carson chose books on animals, nature, and science, reflecting his interests. Carson reports that while he was a "horrible student in the traditionally academic subjects, I excelled in fifth-grade science" (Carson 1990, p. 37). As his science reading expanded, he "became the fifth-grade expert in anything of a scientific nature" (p. 37).

☐ *Carson's mother required him to read two books per week, books that he chose.*

Carson credits reading with improving his reading comprehension and vocabulary, which affected all his academic work, reporting that he became "the best student in math when we did story problems" (p. 38). Consistent with the research, reading also improved his spelling: "I kept reading all through the summer, and by the time I began sixth grade I had learned to spell a lot of words without conscious memorization" (p. 39).

☐ *Carson's reading affected all his academic work.*

The initial impetus his mother provided led to dramatic results: "As I continued to read, my spelling, vocabulary, and comprehension improved, and my classes became much more interesting. I improved so much that by the time I entered seventh grade . . . I was at the top of the class" (p. 39). Clearly, Carson's mother provided him with just the right amount of direct encouragement; because his reading was self-selected, the intrinsic pleasure of reading soon took over, and direct encouragement was no longer necessary.

☐ *Carson's mother provided him with just the right amount of direct encouragement.*

The critical role of self-selection is confirmed in this report from Carlsen and Sherrill (1988):

As soon as I was progressing through the primary grades I remember a distinct lack of enthusiasm for reading because my mother tried to force books on me which I disliked, either because they were too difficult or they were about subject matter in which I had no interest. My older sister had been extremely fond of horse stories and I could not tolerate them (p. 138).

Of course, encouragement only works if readers have access to books, and Rucker's research, discussed above, suggests that in many cases access is enough.

Other Factors

Other factors affect how much reading children do. Possibilities that merit additional research include:

Peer pressure: Appleby and Conner (1965), in their description of a one-semester free reading elective high school English course, informally observed that what students read was heavily influenced by what their peers were reading. Some students, in fact, felt compelled to read what their friends were reading and ignored their own interests. Wendelin and Zinck (1983) asked fifth graders why they selected the books they did. Sixty-nine percent responded that they relied more on friends' recommendations than on teachers' recommendations.

☐ *Young people's reading choices are influenced by their peers.*

Book display: Morrow (1982) reported that good kindergarten and nursery school teachers know just what book store owners know: When library corners have "attracting features," posters, bulletin boards, and displays related to children's literature, children show more interest in books.

☐ *Book displays help.*

□ *Children prefer paperback books to hardback books.*

Paperbacks: Lowrey and Grafft (1965) compared two groups of fourth graders, one reading hardcover books and the other reading paperback versions of the same books (the books were "known to be popular with children and teachers"). The paperback group showed a dramatic improvement in attitude toward books and reading, while the hardcover group showed no significant change. Other studies showing that children prefer paperbacks include Ross (1978), Wendelin and Zinck (1983), and Campbell, Griswald, and Smith (1988). Also, the successful *Hooked on Books* experiment (Fader 1976) emphasized paperbacks.

Jim Trelease, the author of *The Read-Aloud Handbook* (Trelease 1982), has some interesting suggestions on how parents can encourage reading. In a recent interview (Carter 1988), Trelease recommended "the three B's": Book ownership: "Again and again, I meet people who tell me that name of a special book they owned and didn't have to share. . . ." Book rack: Trelease suggests keeping reading materials in book racks in the bathroom. Bed lamp: Every child's bedroom should have one, he says. "Even at age 3, you can say to the child: You are old enough to read in bed like Mom and Dad."

□ *Trelease's three B's:*
  • *book ownership*
  • *book racks*
  • *bed lamps*

□ *Don't forget booktalks.*

In addition, teachers have used booktalks (see, e.g., Duggins 1976) and authors' visits (e.g., Reed 1985) to encourage reading.

Light Reading: Comic Books

□ *The power of comic book reading: The Jim Shooter story.*

On a November day in 1957 I found myself standing in front of Miss Grosier's first grade class in Hillcrest Elementary School, trying to think of a really good word. She had us playing this game in which each kid had to offer up a word to the class, and for every classmate who couldn't spell your word, you got a point—provided of course that you could spell the word. Whoever got the most points received the coveted gold star.

"Bouillabaisse," I said, finally.

"You don't even know what that is," Miss Grosier scolded.

"It's fish soup."

"You can't spell that."

"Can too."

"Come here. Write it." She demanded.

I wrote it. She looked it up, and admitted that it was, indeed, correct.

Easiest gold star I ever won. And right here, right now, I'd like to thank, albeit somewhat belatedly, whoever wrote the Donald Duck comic book in which I found the word bouillabaisse. Also, I'd like to thank my mother who read me that comic book and so many others when I was four and five. . . . I learned to read from those sessions long before I started school. While most of my classmates were struggling with *See Spot Run*, I was reading *Superman*. I knew what indestructible meant, could spell it, and would have cold-bloodedly used it to win another gold star if I hadn't been banned from competition after bouillabaisse . . . (Shooter 1986, p. A85).

The author of this wonderful story is Jim Shooter, former editor-in-chief of the Marvel Comics company. It appeared in the 1986 edition of the *Overstreet Comic Book Price Guide.*

Perhaps the most powerful way of encouraging children to read is by exposing them to light reading, a kind of reading that schools pretend does not exist, and a kind of reading that many

□ *Light reading is how many people learn to read.*

children, for economic or ideological reasons, are deprived of. I suspect that light reading is the way nearly all of us learned to read.

I will focus in this discussion primarily on comic books, partly because there has been more research on comics than on other forms of light reading and partly because comics have been so popular.

Before showing how comics can encourage reading, I present a brief history of comic books in the United States, as well as research that focuses on questions that have been of concern to the public: Are comic book texts "challenging" enough and are they "good English"? Does comic book reading cause any harm? Finally, I bring the discussion around to the original concern: Can comic book reading lead to additional free voluntary reading?

A Brief History

□ *The history of the comic book.*

Comics enjoyed a "Golden Age" from about 1937 to 1955, a time that saw the introduction of such characters as Superman (1938), Batman (1939), Wonder Woman (1941), and Archie (1941). During this time, 90 percent of all elementary school children and 50–80 percent of junior high school students were comic book readers (Slover 1959; Witty and Sizemore 1954; Blakely 1958). Public concern about the impact of comic books on behavior, stimulated in part by Wertham's *Seduction of the Innocent* (1954), resulted in the establishment of the Comics Code, guidelines that one comic book historian referred to as "the most severe form of censorship applied to any mass medium in the United States" (Inge 1985). The result was a decline: "Writers and artists, in an attempt to 'clean up their act,' began to grind out boring and repetitive stories about spooks and funny animals" (Brocka 1979).

The fears about comic books appeared, however, to be unfounded. Research has failed to find a strong relationship between comic book reading and behavior. Hoult (1949) reported that delinquents read more comics and more comics labeled "harmful" and "questionable" than did a comparison group of nondelinquents, but nearly all Hoult's subjects reported reading comic books. Witty (1941) compared the 10 percent of pupils in grades 4 through 6 who read the most comics with the 10 percent who read the least, and found that the two groups "received almost the same average marks and were considered by their teachers to be about equally well-adjusted and effective in social relationships" (p. 108). Lewin (1953, cited in Witty and Sizemore 1955) reported similar results.

□ *Comic book reading is not responsible for antisocial behavior.*

The recovery, the "Silver Age" of comic books, began in 1961, with the publication of Marvel Comics' *Fantastic Four,* followed in 1962 by what may have been the most important event in comic book history in the United States: the first appearance of Spider-Man. Under Stan Lee's leadership, Marvel developed the first superheroes with problems. Spider-Man, for example, has problems that the Superman and Batman of the 1940s and 1950s never imagined—financial problems, romance problems, lack of direction, and a lack of self-esteem.[2]

There is clear evidence that the Silver Age is still going strong. The number of comic book shops in the United States increased from about 100 in the mid-1970s to about 4,000 in 1987, while the annual sales of comic books (not including sales of

☐ *Comic book reading has become popular again.*

used comics) have increased from $200 million in 1983 to $350 million in 1987 (*Los Angeles Herald Examiner*, October 4, 1987). In 1991, McKenna, Kear, and Ellsworth, using a stratified sample of children from 95 school districts in 38 states, reported that the percentage of elementary school children reading comic books in the United States is substantial: For boys, the range is from 69 percent (grade 1) to 75 percent (grade 6), while for girls the range is from 50 percent (grade 6) to 60 percent (grade 1). This is less comic book readership than during the Golden Age of comics, but it is a considerable amount. (The authors also reported that over 75 percent of the children read the newspaper funnies.)

Comic Books and Language Development

Wertham, in *Seduction of the Innocent,* asserted that comic book reading interfered with learning to read and with language development, claiming that "severe reading difficulties and maximum comic book reading go hand in hand, that far from being a help to reading, comic books are a causal and reinforcing factor in children's reading disorders" (p. 130).

☐ *Claims that reading comic books retards reading ability are unfounded.*

Wertham's claims have not been supported. Research done on comic book texts and on the impact of comic book reading on language development and school performance suggests that comic books are not harmful. Moreover, there is considerable evidence that comic books can and do lead to more "serious" reading.

Comic Texts

Comics, first of all, contain a substantial amount of reading volume. R. L. Thorndike (1941) found that currently popular comic books contained about 10,000 words each and concluded that

> the child who reads a comic book once a month through the school year . . . gets about as much wordage of reading as he gets from even the fourth or fifth grade reader. In view of the need of the upper elementary school and junior high school pupil for a large volume of reading and vocabulary-building experience, this source should not be neglected (p. 110).

According to my own estimates, current comics contain far fewer words, averaging about 2,000 per issue (not counting advertisements). This is still a significant amount: One comic a week would mean about 100,000 words per year, about 10 percent of the average yearly reading volume of middle-class children (Anderson, Wilson, and Fielding 1988).

□ *Reading 1 comic book a week would mean reading 100,000 words a year.*

Thorndike's analysis also revealed, contrary to popular opinion, that very little of the vocabulary in comic books was "objectionable." He found only 649 words in four comics (total = 41,000 words) that did not occur in E. L. Thorndike's *Teacher's Word Book of 20,000 Words;* of these 649 words, only 10 percent were classified as "vulgar" slang (e.g., "awk," "betcha," "conk"). This figure underestimates the amount of slang in comics, Thorndike points out, because many standard words are used with slang meanings (e.g., "rod," "joint," etc.): "But even when this is allowed for, one hardly gets the feeling that the language of these particular magazines was excessively

□ *The vocabulary used in comic books is not substandard.*

slangy " (p. 112). This analysis was done 50 years ago, but Thorndike's conclusions would certainly hold true today, as we will see below.

Several studies of comic book reading difficulty have been done. Thorndike (1941) used the Lorge formula and reported that the popular *Superman* and *Batman* comics were written at about the fifth- or sixth-grade level. Wright (1979) used the Fry formula and evaluated a wider range of comics. Wright's findings for superhero comics (e.g., *Superman, The Incredible Hulk*) are consistent with Thorndike's, while other comics are far easier, as shown in table 2.2.[3]

If readability scores have any validity, Thorndike's and Wright's analyses show that comics can be at a respectable level of difficulty. By way of comparison, best sellers in 1974 ranged in readability from grade 6 to grade 10, with a mean readability score of 7.4 (Schulze 1976, cited in Monteith 1980).

To see how sophisticated comic dialogue can get, consider these examples. The first is from Marvel's *Fantastic Four*. In this scene, Reed Richards, a master scientist (a.k.a. Mr. Fantastic), is explaining to his wife Sue Richards (a.k.a. The Invisible Woman) how the villain Psycho-Man operates.

□ *Comic book texts can be complex.*

> The Psycho-Man has a vast technology at his command, darling, but he had traditionally used it to only one end: to manipulate emotions. Everything he does is designed to create conflicting, confusing emotional stimuli for his intended victims (*The Fantastic Four*, no. 283, 1985, p. 21).

Table 2.2
Reading Level of Comic Books (1978)

Title	Readability Grade level 3 samples			Avg.
The Amazing Spider-Man #187	7.4	3.0	2.8	4.4
Archie #274	2.0	1.7	1.7	1.8
Batman #299	7.9	4.0	8.5	6.4
Bugs Bunny #201	2.9	1.9	1.7	2.1
Casper the Friendly Ghost #200	1.9	1.7	1.7	1.8
Chip and Dale #55	2.9	1.9	1.8	2.2
Dennis the Menace #158	2.8	3.0	4.7	3.5
The Incredible Hulk #74	5.5	9.2	1.9	5.5
Mighty Mouse #53	1.9	3.3	1.9	2.4
Sad Sack #265	2.4	1.9	1.9	2.1
Spidey Super Stories	2.7	1.8	1.9	2.1
Star Hunters #7	6.0	7.3	3.3	5.5
Star Wars #16	7.5	7.4	3.3	6.1
Superman #329	7.3	8.3	3.5	6.4
Tarzan #18	7.6	4.4	4.5	5.5
Tom and Jerry #311	1.9	2.0	1.8	1.9
Wonder Woman #245	5.5	5.5	3.5	4.8
Woody Woodpecker #172	2.4	2.4	3.0	3.1
Yogi Bear #7	3.2	3.5	2.4	3.0

☐ *Table 2.2 shows that comic books have a wide variety of reading levels.*

Source: G. Wright, "The Comic Book: A Forgotten Medium in the Classroom," *Reading Teacher* 33 (1979). Reprinted with permission of Gary Wright and the International Reading Association.

In Marvel's *Secret Wars* no. 1, several super-heroes speculate as to how they were involuntarily transported to another planet:

> Captain Marvel: H-how'd we get here? I mean one minute we're checking out this giant whatchamacallit in Central Park, then "poof," the final frontier.

> Mr. Fantastic: This much I can tell you, Captain Marvel—this device apparently caused sub-atomic particle dissociation, reducing us as we entered to proto-matter, which it stored until it teleported us here, to pre-set coordinates in space, where it reassembled us inside a self-generated life support environment.

> The Incredible Hulk: That's obvious, Richards! (*Secret Wars*, no. 1, p. 2).

Deborah Krashen has pointed out to me that if teachers are looking for high-interest/low-vocabulary reading for older students, they can't do better than *Archie*. *Archie* is about high-school-age students, but according to Wright's data, it is written at the second-grade level. In addition, after 50 years, Archie and his friends are still in high school, certainly the longest incarceration in the history of education. This is good news for students and teachers, because it means that there are plenty of used *Archie* comics around.

☐ *Teachers should consider comics as a source for high-interest/low-vocabulary reading.*

Experiments with Comic Book Reading

Two sustained silent reading studies using comic books have been published. In a 15-week study using fifth graders, Sperzl (1948) found no difference between sustained silent reading groups reading comics and a group reading other material in reading comprehension and vocabulary

☐ *Two sustained silent reading studies have been done with comic books.*

growth, and all groups showed acceptable gains. Perhaps the most interesting finding in Sperzl's study is how much the children enjoyed reading comic books. Sperzl reported that "the period was eagerly looked forward to . . . as far as the rest of the world was concerned, it simply did not exist for these boys and girls" (p. 111).

Arlin and Roth (1978) compared third graders reading "educational" (e.g., classic) comics with another group reading "high-interest" books. Both groups gained in reading comprehension. Although "poor readers" gained more from book reading, poor readers reading comic books still matched expected growth, gaining .26 years in 10 weeks.

We can interpret both studies as showing that comic book reading is at least as beneficial as other reading. Both studies, however, were short term (recall the review of in-school free reading studies done in Chapter 1; in-school free reading is clearly more effective when durations are longer), and comic book readers in the Arlin and Roth study read classic comics.[4]

A number of studies confirm that long-term comic book readers, those who continue to read comics after the early grades, are at least equal to noncomic readers in reading, language development, and overall school achievement (Witty 1941; Heisler 1947; Blakely 1958; Swain 1978; Greaney 1980; Anderson, Wilson, and Fielding 1988). Even children who read almost nothing but comic books do not score significantly below average in reading comprehension (Greaney 1980).

□ *Long-term comic book readers maintain an acceptable language development rate.*

An exclusive diet of comic books will probably develop adequate but not advanced levels of competence in language and literacy development.

☐ *However, comic books alone will not develop advanced readers.*

☐ *Comics can serve as a conduit to heavier reading.*

There is good evidence, however, that such reading habits are unusual; in general, long-term comic book readers do as much book reading as noncomic book readers (Witty 1941; Heisler 1947; Bailyn 1959; Swain 1978) and the results of one study suggest they do more (Blakely 1958). Moreover, there is evidence that light reading can serve as a conduit to heavier reading. It can help readers not only develop the linguistic competence for harder reading but can also develop an interest in books.

Comics as a Conduit

One research study and several case histories show that comic book reading can lead to additional book reading. Dorrell and Carroll (1981) placed comic books in a junior high school library, but did not allow them to circulate; students had to come to the library to read the comics. Dorrell and Carroll then compared the circulation of noncomic material and total library use during the 74 days comics were in the library, and the 57 days before they were available. The presence of comics resulted in a dramatic 82 percent increase in library use (traffic) and a 30 percent increase in circulation of noncomic material (table 2.3).

Dorrell and Carroll also reported that the presence of comics in the library did not result in any negative comments from parents, and that teachers, school administrators, and library staff members supported and encouraged the idea of comic books in the library.

Several case histories support the view that light reading is the way many, if not most, children learn to read and develop a taste for reading.

Table 2.3
Effects of Including Comic Books in a Junior
High School Library

	Precomic Period	Comic Period[a]
Number of students who used library[b] (daily average)	272.61	496.38
Circulation (daily average)	77.49	100.99

a. Precomic period = 54 days; comic period = 74 days.
b. Does not include students brought to the library by teachers for class assignments.

Source: Adapted from L. Dorrell and E. Carroll, "Spider-Man at the Library," *School Library Journal* 27 (1981).

□ *General library use increased when comic books were available for circulation.*

Haugaard (1973) writes of her experiences with comic books:

> As the mother of three boys, who, one after the other, were notoriously unmotivated to read and had to be urged, coaxed, cajoled, threatened and drilled in order even to stay in the super slow group in reading, I wish to thank comic books for being a conduit, if not a contribution, to culture.
>
> The first thing which my oldest boy read because he wanted to was a comic book . . . (p. 84).

□ *Comic books lead to other reading.*

Despite her initial reluctance, Haugaard bought her son comics, reasoning that

> as long as these things appealed to him where all other printed matter had failed, I let him read all he wanted. The words he learned to read here could be used in other reading material too and

perhaps his skill would lure him beyond this level (p. 84).

The results were startling:

> He devoured what seemed to be tons of the things.... The motivation these comics provided was absolutely phenomenal and a little bit frightening. My son would snatch up a new one and, with feverish and ravenous eyes, start gobbling it wherever he was—in the car on the way home from the market, in the middle of the yard, walking down the street, at the dinner table. All his senses seemed to shut down and he became a simple visual pipeline (p. 85).

Comics did indeed lead to other reading. After a year or two, Haugaard's eldest son gave his collection away to his younger brother (who now "pores over the comic books lovingly"), and Haugaard notes that "he is far more interested now in reading Jules Verne and Ray Bradbury, books on electronics and science encyclopedias" (p. 85).

Haugaard's experience is consistent with the rest of the literature. Her sons' absorption in comics is identical to the reaction Sperzl's students had (see "Experiments with Comic Book Reading" above), and the eldest son's interest in other kinds of reading agrees with the studies mentioned earlier showing that comic book reading does not replace or eliminate book reading. (It should be pointed out that the results of these studies suggest that Haugaard's eldest son need not have given up comics in order to enjoy other books.)

□ *Autobiographical examples attest to the value of light reading.*

Mark Mathabane, in his autobiographical account of his youth in South Africa (Mathabane 1986), mentions comic books as making an important contribution to his acquisition of English and his desire to read. Mathabane had had limited exposure to English until his grandmother began to work for a friendly English-speaking family outside the impoverished ghetto where Mathabane and his family lived:

> Not long after she started working for the Smiths, she began bringing home stacks of comic books: *Batman and Robin, Richie Rich, Dennis the Menace, The Justice League of America, Tarzan of the Apes, Sherlock Holmes, Mysteries, Superman, The Incredible Hulk, Thor - God of Thunder, The Fantastic Four* and *Spider-Man* (p. 170).

Mathabane's reaction was similar to that of Haugaard's son:

> Having never owned a comic book in my life, I tirelessly read them over and over again, the parts I could understand. Such voracious reading was like an anesthesia, numbing me to the harsh life around me. Soon comic books became the joy of my life, and everywhere I went I took one with me: to the river, to a soccer game, to the lavatory, to sleep, to the store and to school, where I would hide it under the desk, reading it furtively when the teacher was busy at the blackboard ... (p. 170).

Mathabane credits comics with helping to bring his English to a level where he could begin to read and appreciate English books:

> Midway into my eleventh year, Granny started bringing home strange-looking books and toys. The books, which she said were Mrs. Smith's son's schoolbooks, bore no resemblance whatsoever to the ones we used at my school. Their names were as strange to me as their contents: *Pinocchio, Aesop's Fables* and the fairy tales of the brothers Grimm. At this point, because of reading comics, my English had improved to a level where I could read simple sentences. I found the books enthralling (p. 170).

M. Thomas Inge, a professor of the humanities, remarks that comics were clearly a conduit for him and others: "For my generation, it was the comic book that led directly to the printed page" (Inge 1985, p. 5). Professor Inge has clearly not given up reading comics. His essays on comic books (Inge 1985) are informative and scholarly. This writer's experience is similar: I was in the low reading group in the second grade. My father encouraged comic book reading, and improvement soon followed. There is thus every reason to hypothesize that comics can serve as a conduit to additional reading.

☐ *"For my generation, it was the comic book that led directly to the printed page."*

Conclusions

The case for comics is a good one:

☐ *Comics are*
  • *linguistically appropriate*
  • *not detrimental to reading development*
  • *conduits to book reading*

• The texts of comics are linguistically appropriate, and pictures can help make the texts comprehensible.[5]

• Research shows that comics have no negative effect on language development and school achievement.

• Comic book readers do at least as much book reading as non-comic book readers. There is, moreover, suggestive evidence that comics may serve as a conduit to book reading.

Light Reading: The Teen Romance

☐ *The teen romance is a popular formula novel.*

Another example of light reading that can encourage additional reading is the teen romance. Parrish (1983) provides this characterization:

> Most of the teen romance books are written to a formula. The central character is a girl, 15 to 16 years old, and the story is always told from her

viewpoint. One or more boys, 17 to 18 years old are also needed. The setting is usually contemporary and familiar, such as a small town. First love is a favorite plot focus.

The joys of falling in love, the anxiety it engenders, the pain and growth of problems met, and the inevitable happy ending are all standard. However, these romances exclude sexual situations, profanity, or perversions. The conflict is usually about the heroine's feelings—insecurity, uncertainty, unpopularity, inferiority, pleasure/pain, a struggle for independence. Dialogue generally carries the action, while characterization is revealed through the romantic interaction and problems . . . (p. 611).

Like comic books, teen romances are big business. According to Sutton (1985), the most successful series, *Sweet Valley High,* had sold close to 10 million copies after 25 volumes (at the time of this writing, the series was up to number 78). Also, teen romances are read by many, if not most, girls in junior high school and high school. Parrish and Atwood (1985) surveyed 250 junior and senior high school girls in the Phoenix metropolitan area, and reported that during the school year, 50 percent of the eighth graders said they had read from one to five teen romances, and 100 percent of the ninth graders had read at least five. Also, "an astonishing 12% of the twelfth graders had read in excess of thirty novels this school year" (p. 24).

☐ *They are extremely popular with teenage girls.*

Although there has been little research on teen romances, the results are quite similar to those of comic book research:

☐ *They parallel comics in their beneficial effect on literacy.*

Teen romances appear to have linguistically acceptable texts, ranging from grade 4 to grade 7. *Sweet Valley Twins* is written at grade 4 reading level, *Sweet Dream Romances,* written for girls ages

☐ *Reading levels range from grades 4 to 7.*

10 to 15, is at the fifth-grade level, while the *Sweet Valley High* series, for age 12 and older, is written at the sixth-grade level. *Caitlin,* a "love trilogy" by Francine Pascal, ranges from grade 5 to 7 reading level. By way of comparison, recall that the mean readability level of best sellers in 1974 was calculated to be grade 7.4 (see "Comic Texts" above).

Reading teen romances does not seem to prevent other kinds of reading. Parrish and Atwood (1985) found that "students who read the romance novels read many other kinds of literature also" (p. 25).

Teen romances appear to bring students into the library. According to Parrish and Atwood, eighth and ninth graders get their romance novels equally from friends, bookstores, and school libraries. Tenth graders favor drug/grocery stores and the school library. Twelfth graders showed the most diversity: Over half got their books from friends and the public library, 37 percent from bookstores and the school library, with little use of home and drug/grocery stores. Thus, despite the easy availability of teen romances, the school library still plays a significant role as a source of reading for this genre.

☐ *Reading teen romances generally promotes reading.*

There is evidence that reading teen romances promotes reading. The following, quoted by Parrish (1983), sounds very much like Haugaard's report of how comic books stimulate reading. The writer is a 14-year-old girl: "I am the kind of person who hates to read, but when my mother brought home a Silhouette book for me to read, I just couldn't put it down" (p. 615).

Just as there has been concern about the content of comic books, there is concern about the content of teen romances. There has been no research on the behavioral effects of teen romances, but concerned teachers and parents may be interested in reading some thoughtful reviews. Sutton (1985) gives the teen romance cautious approval, suggesting that while we regard "the lesser lights of paperback fiction as the competition" (p. 29), they have some merit:

□ *There is no research on the behavioral effects of reading teen romances.*

> Characterization is minimal, the writing is less than graceful ("They were all being so polite and civilized the twins thought they would throw up.") and even romance is overshadowed by the soap opera suspense. But it does work: the bare bones plots, hokey and hoary, move. The links between successive volumes are clever, and you really want to know (the way you really want to know about "Dynasty's" Alexis Colby) what Jessica is going to pull next (p. 27).

The case for teen romances, so far, is a good one.

Is Light Reading Enough?

□ *Probably not.*

It is sensible to suppose that what is read matters. Despite the benefits of light reading, a diet of only light reading will probably not lead to advanced levels of development. Only a few studies bear on this issue, but they suggest that reading comprehension and vocabulary development are related to what is read.

□ *Studies show that reading ability is related to reading material.*

Rice (1986) reported that adults with better vocabularies "tended to read more sophisticated materials," such as technical journals, history, literary magazines, and science magazines. Hafner, Palmer, and Tullos (1986) found that better readers (top one-half on a reading comprehension test) in the ninth grade tended to prefer "complex fiction" (historical fiction, science fiction, mystery, adventure, personal development, personal insight), while "poor readers" (bottom one-half) tended to prefer "how-to-do-it" books, science books, westerns, books on religion, biography, hobby books, and books on art, music, and history. Southgate, Arnold, and Johnson (1981) found that seven- to nine-year-olds who were better readers preferred adventure books, while "funny books" were more popular with less advanced readers.

Thorndike (1973), in his large-scale study of reading comprehension in 15 countries, reported that for 14-year-olds the types of reading that correlated best with reading comprehension ability were, in order, 1) humor, 2) history and biography, science fiction, myths, and legends, and 3) adventure and current events. Thorndike also reported that by the end of secondary school the pattern had changed somewhat: While sports, love stories, and school stories were negatively correlated with reading comprehension, history and biography, technical science, and philosophy and religion showed the strongest positive correlation.

There is some agreement among the studies; science fiction and adventure books seem to be consistently preferred by good readers. There are also some contradictions: Good readers, according to Thorndike, prefer history and religious books, but in the Hafner, Palmer, and Tullos study, poor readers preferred these topics. (An obvious problem with relating reading growth to genre is that there may be quite a bit of variation in complexity within one kind of reading. Clearly, research in this area has just begun.)

As noted earlier, Greaney (1980) identified a group of "predominately comic book readers," fifth-grade children who did far more comic book reading than book reading. These children were not significantly below the group average in reading comprehension, but were not as proficient as children classified as "predominately book readers."

The results of these studies do not imply that light reading is to be avoided. As argued earlier, light reading can serve as a conduit to heavier reading: It provides both the motivation for more reading and the linguistic competence that makes harder reading possible. Reassuring and supporting evidence comes from studies that show that many children who do extensive free reading eventually choose what experts have decided are "good books" (Schoonover 1938), and studies show that readers gradually expand their reading interests as they read more (LaBrant 1958). Also, several studies show that books that children select on their own are typically harder than the reading material assigned by teachers (Southgate, Arnold, and Johnson 1981; Bader, Veatch, and Eldridge 1987).[6]

☐ *Light reading is not to be avoided but should be used as a conduit to more serious reading.*

Notes

1. But see Wollner (1949), who reported very low correlations between the number of books in the home library and how much reading children did in grades 7, 8, and 9 (r = .11). Nearly all the children in this sample, however, lived in homes with large book collections, averaging about 750 books, and ranging from 50 to 3,000 books.

2. It should be noted that Peter Parker, a.k.a. Spider-Man, married Mary Jane Watson in July 1987. At the time of this writing, Mr. and Mrs.

Parker are happily married, thus solving at least one of Spider-Man's problems.

☐ *Note 3 discusses the Fry formula.*

3. The Fry formula is based on three random samples of 100 words. These samples can vary quite a bit. Note, for example, the variability in the three samples for *The Incredible Hulk* in table 2.2 (5.5, 9.2, 1.9). Daniel Krashen has suggested to me that the 9.2 sample may have been based on the speech of Bruce Banner, the Hulk's alter ego. Banner is a research scientist, and his speech reflects his profession.

4. Although classic comics are probably more acceptable to parents and teachers, there is evidence that they are not all that popular with children. Wayne (1954) asked 297 seventh-grade students to indicate which comic types they preferred; each student was asked to choose four from a list of 15. Classic comics ranked ninth out of 15. When children are asked which comics they prefer, without a list to choose from, classic comics are never mentioned (for a review of these studies, see Witty and Sizemore 1954).

☐ *Note 5 discusses pictures versus text in comic books.*

5. There has been some concern that the pictures in comic books will allow children to ignore the text and might actually interfere with learning to read (Wertham 1954). According to language acquisition theory, however, pictures can actually help, because they can provide clues that shed light on the meaning of an unfamiliar word or grammatical structure—they can, in other words, help make input more comprehensible (Krashen 1985b).

But some children do ignore the text and only look at the pictures. Bailyn (1959) found that 27 percent of the fifth- and sixth-grade boys she observed reading comic books "concentrated mainly on the pictures." In their sustained silent reading study, Arlin and Roth (1978) reported that poor readers appeared to do more picture reading of comic books than good readers did.

Why are some children picture readers? At first glance, the picture reading syndrome is puzzling, because pictures do not tell the whole story in most comics, and children do not typically ignore print in their environment. Here are some possibilities:

A difficult text combined with attractive pictures. While readers can tolerate some "noise" in texts, too many unknown elements will discourage attempts at comprehension (Frebody and Anderson 1983). A second grader may not even try to read the relatively complex text and often subtle story line of comics such as *X-Men,* but might find the pictures of great interest.

Mistaken assumptions about reading. Some picture readers may be able to read substantial portions of the text but do not attempt to read. It is possible that their incorrect assumptions about reading discourage these children from trying to read. Because of "reading lessons" in school, they may have the mistaken impression that in order to read, they need to know every word in the text. Such an assumption sets up a defeating sequence of events: The reader reads less, and as a result has less of a chance to develop reading ability and acquire more language.

These are only possibilities. Frank Smith has pointed out to me that if they are true, it does not follow that picture reading can be cured by denying the child comic books. More comic reading, not less, may be the solution. With more exposure, the

□ *Picture readers may not be cured by denying access to comic books.*

child's interest in the story might stimulate attempts at reading.

6. No studies, to my knowledge, have attempted to find a relationship between what is read and writing style. Such a relationship surely exists, because different styles have different linguistic characteristics. Smith (1988b) has noted this, and advises: "To learn to write for newspapers, you must read newspapers; textbooks about them will not suffice. For magazines, browse through magazines rather than through correspondence courses on magazine writing. To write poetry, read it. For the conventional style of memoranda (schools), consult the school file."

Nevertheless, it is probably true that reading anything at all will help all writing, to at least some extent. Although there are clearly different styles of prose, there is also considerable overlap among styles (see, e.g., Biber 1986): So-called narrative style, has, for example, some (but not all) of the characteristics of formal, expository style. Reading novels, therefore, will not make you a competent essayist; you will have to read lots of essays to fully develop the essay-type style. But reading novels will give you at least some of the features of essay style; a novel reader will write a much better essay, stylistically, than someone who has read little of anything.

☐ *Note 6 discusses reading and its relation to writing style.*

Other Issues and Conclusions 3

Questions about the relationship of free voluntary reading and other factors involved in literacy are inevitable. Some of the more important questions addressed in this chapter are

1. What are the limits of FVR?
2. When is direct instruction most effective?
3. What is the relationship of reading to writing?
4. What is the effect of television viewing on literacy?

The Limits of Reading

Even with massive free voluntary reading of appropriate texts, complete acquisition of the conventions of writing may not take place; even very well-read people may have gaps in their competence. Typically, these gaps are small, and many readers will recognize them as problems they experience. Here are some examples:

☐ *Even with extensive FVR, gaps in literacy may remain.*

Spelling demons: Words like "committment" (or is it "commitment"?) and "independence" (or is it "independance"?).

Punctuation: Does the comma go inside or outside the quotation mark?

Grammar: Subject-verb agreement in sentences such as: A large group of boys is (are?) expected to arrive tomorrow.

These errors usually do not make much of a difference in terms of communication. "Independance," for example, communicates the idea just as well as "independence." Obeying the rules, however, is important for cosmetic reasons; readers often find written language containing errors irritating, and this reaction can detract from the writer's message.

Why do well-read readers have gaps? What prevents full acquisition of the written language? One explanation is that not all the print is attended to; that is, successful reading for meaning does not require full use of everything that appears on the page. It has been demonstrated (Goodman 1982; Smith 1988a) that fluent readers generate hypotheses about the text they are about to read—based on what they have read already, their knowledge of the world, and their knowledge of language—and only use those aspects of print they need to confirm their hypotheses. For example, most readers can guess what the last word of this sentence is going to __. Good readers don't need to fully and carefully perceive the "be" at the end of the sentence in order to understand it; they just need to see enough to confirm that it is there.

☐ *Good readers do not attend to everything that appears on the page.*

Thus, competent readers do not pay attention to every detail on the page, and they may fail to acquire the its/it's distinction or whether certain words end in -ence or -ance. These tiny gaps are, in my view, a small price to pay for fluent and efficient reading.

Even those aspects of print that are attended to and understood may not be acquired. Several researchers have hypothesized that affective factors may be responsible. Dulay and Burt (1977; see also Dulay, Burt, and Krashen 1982) have suggested that for language acquisition to occur, language acquirers need to be "open" to the input or have a low Affective Filter. When language acquirers are anxious, or put on the defensive, the input may be understood, but it will not reach those parts of the brain that are responsible for language acquisition (what Chomsky has called the "language acquisition device"; see Chomsky 1965). A block, the Affective Filter, will keep the input out.

□ The "Affective Filter" prevents input from reaching the "language acquisition device."

Smith (1988b) has pointed out that a great deal of learning occurs effortlessly, when learners consider themselves to be potential members of certain groups, or "clubs," and expect to learn. Teenagers, for example, learn the elaborate dress code, slang, and behavior patterns of their peers not by deliberate study but by observing others and deciding that they want to be like them. Similarly, Smith argues, when readers conclude that they are potential members of the "literacy club," people who use reading and writing, they "read like writers," and absorb the enormous amount of knowledge that writers possess. Smith's idea is quite consistent with the Affective Filter hypothesis: Considering oneself a member or potential member of the literacy club results in a lower Affective Filter, with more of the input reaching the language acquisition device.[1]

□ When readers consider themselves to be potential members of "the literacy club," they absorb the enormous amount of information that writers possess.

What can be done to fill these tiny gaps, those that remain even after massive reading and after entrance into the literacy club? We do, unfortunately, need to be concerned, because society's standards for writing accuracy are 100 percent: Errors in spelling, punctuation, and grammar are not tolerated in writing intended to be read by others.

Direct teaching and the use of grammar handbooks and dictionaries can help us fill at least part of the gap. Such conscious learning of language is very limited, however, and needs to be used with

□ Direct teaching can help fill some of the gap.

caution—an excessive concern with form or correctness while trying to work out new ideas in writing can be very disruptive. Experienced writers know this and limit their "editing" to the final draft, after their ideas have been worked out on the page (see, e.g., Sommers 1980). It also seems reasonable to expect that only more mature students will be able to develop extensive conscious knowledge; it might be most efficient to delay this kind of direct teaching until high school.

☐ *Direct teaching may be most efficient for older students.*

Given extensive free reading, however, and a genuine invitation to join the literacy club, readers will acquire nearly all of the conventions of writing. With enough reading, good grammar, good spelling, and good style will be part of them, absorbed or acquired effortlessly.

Writing

Writing deserves more space than I am giving it here. My goal, however, is not to provide a complete survey of what is known about writing and how writing ability develops, but to make two crucial points:

1. Writing style does not come from writing, but from reading.

2. Actual writing can help us solve problems and make us smarter.

Writing Style Comes from Reading

The research reviewed earlier strongly implies that we learn to write by reading. To be more precise, we acquire writing style, the special language of writing, by reading. We have already seen plenty of evidence that this is so: In Chapter

1 we saw that children who participate in free reading programs write better (e.g., Elley and Mangubhai 1983; McNeil in Fader 1976), and those who report they read more write better (e.g., Kimberling et al. 1988 as reported in Krashen 1978, 1984; Applebee 1978; Alexander 1986; Salyer 1987; Janopoulos 1986; Kaplan and Palhinda 1981; Applebee et al. 1990).

There are other reasons to suspect that writing style comes from reading. The "complexity argument" (Chapter 1) applies to writing as well: All the ways in which "formal" written language differs from more informal language are too complex to be learned one rule at a time. Even though readers can recognize good writing, researchers have not succeeded in completely describing just what it is that makes a "good" writing style good. It is, therefore, sensible to suppose that writing style is not consciously learned, but is largely absorbed, or subconsciously acquired, from reading.

□ *Formal written language is too complex to be learned one rule at a time.*

According to much common wisdom, we learn to write by actually writing. The reading hypothesis asserts that this is not true, at least as far as style is concerned. Smith (1988) tells us why we do not learn to write by writing:

□ *We do not learn to write by writing.*

> I thought the answer [to how we learn to write] must be that we learn to write by writing until I reflected upon how little anyone writes in school, even the eager students, and how little feedback is provided. . . . No one writes enough to learn more than a small part of what writers need to know . . . (p. 19).

The research confirms Smith's reflections. Actual writing in school appears to be infrequent. Applebee, Langer, and Mullis (1986) asked students how many essays and reports they had written over six weeks for any school subject. Only 18.6 percent of the fourth graders wrote more than 10, while only 7.8 percent of the eleventh graders wrote more than 10. Writing outside of school is also not frequent: Applebee et al.'s eleventh-grade group did the most out-of-school writing, but only 17.4 percent kept diaries, 37.3 percent said they wrote letters to friends, and 74.8 percent said they wrote notes and messages at least weekly. (See also Applebee et al. 1990 and Snow, Barnes, Chandler, Goodman, and Hemphill 1991 for similar results.)

Research by Rice (1986) allows us to make at least a crude comparison of writing and reading frequency outside of school. Rice probed reading and writing behavior of several groups, and I present one of them (high verbal adults) as a representative example. These subjects reported 15.1 hours per week in "total reading," but only two hours per week in writing (1.9 hours for "short writing" and .1 hours for "long writing"). Assuming even a very slow reading rate (200 words per minute [wpm]) and a very fast writing rate (typing at 60 wpm), this still means that people deal with far more words in reading than in writing (a ratio of 25 to 1). More likely, the true ratio is closer to 150 to 1. Considering the complexity of the system that is to be acquired, these data severely weaken the case for writing as an important source of language acquisition. (See also Evans and Gleadow 1983 for similar estimates of reading and writing frequency.)

The research evidence also shows, in addition, that more writing does not typically lead to better writing. Although some studies show that good writers do more writing than poor writers (see Applebee et al. 1990 and studies summarized in

□ *The actual amount of writing done by a typical student is low.*

□ *People read much more than they write.*

74

Krashen 1984), increasing the amount of writing students do does not increase their writing proficiency. (First language studies include Dressel, Schmid, and Kincaid 1952; Arnold 1964; Varble 1990. Hunting [1967] describes unpublished dissertation research showing that writing quantity is not related to writing quality. For a second language study, see Burger 1989. An exception is Lokke and Wykoff 1948; very small differences were found, however, between college freshmen who wrote two themes per week and those who wrote one theme per week.) In addition, Hillocks (1986), after an extensive review that included unpublished dissertation research, found that writing classes that emphasized free writing did not produce significantly better writing than comparison classes.

☐ *Numerous studies show that increasing writing quantity does not affect writing quality.*

Similarly, Gradman and Hanania (1991) found that while "extracurricular reading" was a strong predictor of TOEFL (Test of English as a Foreign Language) scores among international students (r = .53), frequency of extracurricular writing did not correlate with TOEFL performance. Finally, Foertsch (1992) reported that the amount of journal writing done by fourth-, eighth-, and twelfth-grade students did not clearly relate to their reading comprehension ability. Also, those who wrote more reports on what they had read were not superior in reading comprehension. In both cases, there was a tendency for those who wrote the most and the least to do the worst in reading comprehension, while those who wrote a moderate amount did the best.

Hypothesizing that writing style comes from reading, not from writing, is consistent with what is known about language acquisition: Language

□ *Language acquisition comes from input, not output; from comprehension, not production.*

acquisition comes from input, not output, from comprehension, not production. Thus, if you write a page a day, your writing style or your command of mechanics will not improve. However, other good things may result from your writing, as we shall see in the next section.

What Writing Does

Although writing does not help us develop writing style, writing has other virtues. As Smith has pointed out (1988), we write for at least two reasons. First, and most obvious, we write to communicate with others. But perhaps more important, we write for ourselves, to clarify and stimulate our thinking. Most of our writing, even if we are published authors, is for ourselves.

□ *Writing does help us communicate, but writing is usually done for ourselves.*

As Elbow (1973) has noted, it is difficult to hold more than one thought in mind at a time. When we write our ideas down, the vague and abstract become clear and concrete. When thoughts are on paper, we can see the relationships between them, and can come up with better thoughts. Writing, in other words, can make us smarter.

□ *Writing can help us think through and solve problems.*

Readers who keep a diary or journal know all about this—you have a problem, you write it down, and at least 10 percent of the problem disappears. Sometimes, the entire problem goes away. Here is an example of this happening, a letter written to Ann Landers in 1976:

> Dear Ann: I'm a 26-year-old woman and feel like a fool asking you this question, but—should I marry the guy or not? Jerry is 30, but sometimes he acts like 14. . . .
>
> Jerry is a salesman and makes good money but has lost his wallet three times since I've known

him and I've had to help him meet the payments on his car.

The thing that bothers me most, I think, is that I have the feeling he doesn't trust me. After every date he telephones. He says it's to "say an extra goodnight," but I'm sure he is checking to see if I had a late date with someone else.

☐ *A case in point.*

One night I was in the shower and didn't hear the phone. He came over and sat on the porch all night. I found him asleep on the swing when I went to get the paper the next morning at 6:30 a.m. I had a hard time convincing him I had been in the house the whole time.

Now on the plus side: Jerry is very good-looking and appeals to me physically. Well - that does it. I have been sitting here with this pen in my hand for 15 minutes trying to think of something else good to say about him and nothing comes to mind.

Don't bother to answer this. You have helped more than you will ever know. —Eyes Opened. (Permission granted by Ann Landers and Creators Syndicate.)

Perhaps the clearest experimental evidence showing that writing helps thinking is from a series of studies by Langer and Applebee (1987). High school students were asked to read social studies passages and then study the information in them either by writing an analytic essay on an assigned question relating to the passage, or by using other study techniques (e.g., note taking, answering comprehension questions, writing summaries, "normal" studying without writing). Students were then given a variety of tests on the material in the passages. Langer and Applebee reported that "in general, any kind of written response leads to better performance than does

☐ *Studies show that writing does help thinking.*

77

reading without writing" (p. 130). In their third study, they showed that essay writing did not result in greater retention of information when the reading passage was easy; when the passage they read was difficult, however, essay writers did much better than students using other study techniques. Similar results for the effectiveness of essay writing have been reported by Newell (1984), Marshall (1987), and Newell and Winograd (1989).

Sometimes just a little bit of writing can make a big difference. In Ganguli's study (1989) college mathematics students who devoted three minutes per period to describing in writing an important concept covered in class easily outperformed a comparison group on the semester final exam. For a review of additional research supporting the hypothesis that writing "can make you smarter," see Applebee (1984) and Krashen (1990).

The Effect of Television

□ *It is widely assumed that watching television has a negative effect on reading. Not so.*

It is widely assumed that watching television has a negative effect on reading and other aspects of language. There are at least two commonsense arguments against television. First, watching TV takes time, time that could be spent reading (this is known as the "displacement argument"). The evidence, we will see, does not confirm this claim.

A second argument against television is that TV programs do not provide the kind of input that would stimulate language development. According to the available research, this assertion is true: TV language is not nearly as complex as book language. Nevertheless, a moderate amount of TV watching appears to be harmless; studies show no significant impact of TV watching on tests of literacy and school performance, unless the amount of TV watching is excessive.

Does More Television Mean Less Reading?

The view that television watching displaces reading is a popular one, and a few case histories appear to support it. Some of the college students who wrote reading autobiographies in Carlsen and Sherrill (1988) blamed television for preventing them from becoming readers and, in the following case, for extinguishing their interest in reading: "I continued this avid interest in reading until I was in fifth grade. Then the one-eyed monster, commonly known as television, entered the realms of our living room. . . . To say the least, the television set replaced any book . . ." (p. 138). Nevertheless, the research does not support the displacement hypothesis.

☐ *For some, watching television does replace reading, but not generally.*

When televison is new, it can displace reading. This effect occurs when it is initially introduced into a community (Brown, Cramond, and Wilde 1974), and when viewers are very young (six-year-olds in Gadberry 1980). Some early studies done when television was just introduced in the United States also show that TV watchers read less (Coffin 1948; Maccoby 1951), as did a survey carried out in 1965–1966 of the impact of TV in 14 countries (Robinson 1972).

When television is more established in a community, TV viewers read just as much as nonviewers, however (Himmelweit, Oppenheim, and Vince 1958), and more recent studies done in the United States also show no relationship between television watching and book reading (Schramm, Lyle, and Parker 1961; Robinson 1980; Zuckerman, Singer, and Singer 1980; but see McEvoy and

☐ *Television viewers read just as much as nonviewers.*

Vincent 1980, who found no difference in TV watching between "light" and "heavy" readers but reported that "nonreaders" watched more television).[2]

The finding of no relationship between amount of television watching and amount of free reading may be the result of a balance of two forces. Some studies suggest that television can actually encourage reading: The dramatization of a book on television increases the likelihood that the book will be read (Himmelweit, Oppenheim, and Vince 1958; Busch 1978; Wendelin and Zinck 1983; Campbell, Griswald, and Smith 1988). (It is possible, however, that television does not increase overall reading, but simply "redirects the existing reading choice of an audience" [Beentjes and Van der Voort 1988, p. 392].)

☐ *Sometimes television can stimulate or at least redirect what is read.*

Conversely, it has been argued that television discourages reading and other uses of literacy—television characters are rarely seen reading or writing, or even behaving as if they read and write. As Postman (1983) has pointed out:

> It is quite noticeable that the majority of adults on TV shows are depicted as functionally illiterate, not only in the sense that the content of book learning is absent from what they appear to know but also because of the absence of even the faintest signs of a contemplative habit of mind (p. 12).

The Language of Television

☐ *Television does not provide high-quality linguistic input.*

There does seem to be some basis for the second accusation presented at the beginning of this section: Television does not provide high-quality linguistic input.

Fasick (1973) reported that the language used in children's books was significantly more complicated than the language used in children's television shows. For example, 64 percent of the sentences in books (five books recommended for reading aloud to preschool children) were "complex," compared to 34 percent for television ("Captain Kangaroo" and two cartoons). Moreover, the complex sentences found in the books involved more subordination. In other words, the complex sentences in the books were more complex. Fasick concluded that the language of television was only about as complicated as the speech of average fifth graders.

☐ *The language of children's books is more complex than that of children's television.*

Liberman (1979) analyzed the language used in programs popular in the 1970s. His analysis of sentence complexity is in close agreement with Fasick's results. In addition, Liberman also reported that the quantity of language used on television was low. Of the eight shows Liberman analyzed, the one using the largest number of words, "M.A.S.H.," contained a total of 3,395 words, and only 900 *different* words.

☐ *The quantity of language used on television is low.*

Liberman concluded that "very likely, the lexicon of TV programming is under 5,000 words" (p. 604), a pathetic result when one considers that estimates of first graders' vocabulary size range from 5,500 to 32,000 words (M. Smith 1941; see also note 13, Chapter 1).

Thus, while popular television shows might provide some input of value to beginning language acquirers, they do not compare very well to reading, either in the complexity or amount of language they provide.

Television and Language Development

The impact of television on school-related measures, including reading comprehension, vocabulary, spelling, and "language arts," has been thoroughly studied. Several careful reviews of this research have been done (Williams, Haertel, Haertel, and Walberg 1982; Beentjes and Van der Voort 1988; see also recent studies by Neuman 1988 and Foertsch 1992) and they arrive at similar conclusions:

☐ *TV watching decreases literacy only slightly.*

• The overall impact of television is negative, but slight; in fact, it is hardly detectable. No matter what measures of achievement are examined, more television watching means only slightly reduced performance in reading comprehension, vocabulary, and other school-related measures.

☐ *More television means better school performance but only for moderate amounts of TV watching.*

• Achievement actually increases (slightly) with moderate amounts of TV watching, that is, the more TV, the better subjects do on school-related tests up to about two hours of TV per day. After reaching this threshold, however, the relationship is negative: The more TV, the worse students do, with TV watching showing a clearly negative impact when it exceeds four hours per day (see, e.g., Neuman 1988). Interestingly, increased television watching is associated with better literacy development in English for children acquiring English as a second language (Blosser 1988); this relationship did not hold true for beginners, however, for whom English-language television was probably not comprehensible.

- There is some evidence that television has more negative effects on older students (high school: Neuman 1988), and on higher socio-economic classes (Beentjes and Van der Voort 1988). Also, as one would expect, there is evidence that the impact of television depends on what programs children watch, with lower achievement related to watching entertainment-type and adventure programs (Neuman 1981).[3] In general, however, correlations between what is watched and reading achievement are very modest (Neuman 1981; Degrotsky 1981; Potter 1987).

Summary

Much of what is on television may not be of high quality; nevertheless, television is clearly not the culprit in the "literacy crisis." Although the language of many TV shows is not impressive, there is no clear evidence that TV displaces reading, and there is only a weak negative relationship between TV watching and performance on school-related tests. In fact, a little TV watching appears to be better than none at all and TV watching may be helpful for second language acquisition. It is only when television watching is excessive that a clear negative effect appears.

☐ *Television is not the culprit in the "literacy crisis."*

Phrased slightly differently, it seems that those who do better on tests of language and literacy read more, but watch TV only a little less. Apparently it is not the presence of television that prevents children from reading; more likely, it is the absence of good books.[4]

☐ *The culprit seems to be the absence of good books.*

Conclusions

My conclusions are simple. When children read for pleasure, when they get "hooked on books," they acquire, involuntarily and without conscious effort, nearly all of the so-called "language skills" many people are so concerned about: They will become adequate readers, acquire a large vocabulary, develop the ability to understand and use complex grammatical constructions, develop a good writing style, and become good (but not necessarily perfect) spellers. Although free voluntary reading alone will not ensure attainment of the highest levels of literacy, it will at least ensure an acceptable level. Without it, I suspect that children simply do not have a chance.

☐ *Children who are readers will develop acceptable levels of literacy.*

☐ *Without a reading habit, children simply do not have a chance.*

When second language acquirers read for pleasure, they develop the competence they need to move from the beginning "ordinary conversational" level to a level where they can use the second language for more demanding purposes, such as the serious study of literature, business, and so on. When they read for pleasure, they can continue to improve in their second language without classes, without teachers, without study, and even without people to converse with.[5]

☐ *People acquiring a second language have the best chance for success through reading.*

When we read, we really have no choice—we must develop literacy. We rarely find well-read people who have serious problems with grammar, spelling, and so on. They write acceptably well because they can't help it; they have subconsciously acquired good writing style as well as the conventions of writing.

☐ *Well-read people write well because they have subconsciously acquired good writing style.*

I am not, however, proposing a language program consisting only of free reading. I also recognize the value of reading that is assigned by teachers and recommended by teachers, librarians, and parents. A language arts class, in my view, is primarily a literature class. Assigned reading and free voluntary reading will help each other: Through literature, students will grow intellectually and be exposed to a wider variety of books, which can stimulate more free reading. In fact, one of the ways we know that a literature program is effective is if it results in more free voluntary reading. In turn, free voluntary reading will help build language competence and contribute to intellectual growth, which will make literature more comprehensible and meaningful.

☐ *FVR is not a replacement for the language program. FVR complements language arts classes.*

Our problem in language education, as Frank Smith has pointed out, is that we have confused cause and effect. We have assumed that we first learn language "skills" and then apply these skills to reading and writing. But that is not the way the human brain works. Rather, reading for meaning, reading about things that matter to us, is the cause of literate language development.

☐ *We have confused cause and effect.*

If this view is even partially correct, it means that we need to create a print-rich environment both inside and outside of school. It means that teachers need to be assured that creating such an environment will make their jobs easier, not harder, and will give more satisfying results.[6]

Administrators need to know that when teachers are reading to students, and when teachers are relaxing with a good book during sustained silent reading sessions, teachers are doing their job. Administrators need to know that a print-rich environment is not a luxury but a necessity. (Administrators will be relieved to know that creating a print-rich environment is not excessively expensive: For the price of one computer, a school library

☐ *Creating a print-rich environment is a key.*

can be significantly improved.) Administrators will also be pleased to know that providing a print-rich environment will lead to an easier and more fulfilling day for teachers, with improved student competence in reading and language arts.

☐ *Parents should opt for actual reading rather than using workbooks.*

Parents need to know that children will get far more benefit from being read to, from seeing parents read for pleasure, and from reading comics, magazines, and books, than they will from working through workbooks on sale at the local drugstore.

☐ *FVR is more pleasant for children than skill-based instruction.*

Finally, there is no question that free voluntary reading is more pleasant for the children as well. The research literature is replete with reports of the pleasure children get from free reading (e.g., Schwartzenberg 1962; Carlsen and Sherrill 1988; Nell 1988), as well as the boredom that often accompanies some required reading. While it may not be true that everything that is good for you is pleasant, the most effective way of building literacy happens to be the most pleasant. Clearly, "no pain, no gain" does not apply to literacy development.

Notes

1. Smith's hypothesis explains why some of us cannot seem to write convincingly in certain styles, despite massive reading of texts written in those styles. I have read widely, but seem only to be able to write comfortably in the academic (or at best modified academic) style you are now reading, reflecting the club I have joined. (I have been told that even my personal letters read like journal papers.) Smith's hypothesis also explains, conversely, why reading just a modest amount of authors we admire can influence our writing style.

2. There is some evidence supporting the reasonable hypothesis that what children watch affects how much they read. In agreement with other research, Zuckerman, Singer, and Singer (1980) found no overall relationship between time spent watching TV and time spent reading, but they also found that children who watched more "fantasy violent" programs tended to read less. Schramm, Lyle, and Parker (1961) also reported no relation between TV watching and book reading, but found that children who watch more TV read fewer comic books (see also Murray and Kippax 1978 for similar results).

☐ *What children watch on television influences how much they read.*

3. This is consistent with research showing that children who watch more "violent fantasy" programs do less reading, as mentioned in note 2 above.

4. Cleary (1939) found that the impact of radio in the 1930s was remarkably similar to the impact of television today. Those who did very little radio listening had less interest in reading and those who did a great deal (more than three hours per day) also read fewer books (but read more newspapers and magazines).

Cleary also reported that heavy movie goers, those who attended more than three films per week (5 percent of her sample) read more books and read higher quality books.

☐ *Heavy moviegoers generally are readers.*

5. There are compelling reasons for encouraging the development of literacy via pleasure reading in the first language for second language acquirers. First, if it is true that we "learn to read by reading" (Goodman 1982; Smith 1988a), it is obviously easier to learn to read in a language the reader understands. Thus, it will be easier to learn to read in the primary language. Once the ability

☐ *Learning to read in one language helps us read a second language.*

to read is acquired, there is good evidence that much of this ability transfers to the second language (see, e.g., Cummins 1991).

Second, reading provides knowledge, knowledge of the world as well as subject matter knowledge. The knowledge gained through the first language can make second language input much more comprehensible.

Third, there is reason to suspect that the pleasure reading habit itself transfers. A pleasure reader in the first language will become a pleasure reader in the second language.

Evidence that suggests that reading in the first language is helpful for second language acquisition is the success of bilingual programs that provide literacy development and subject matter teaching in the primary language. Such programs, it has been shown, teach English as well as or better than programs in which children are taught in English all day (Willig 1985; Krashen and Biber 1988).

6. One obvious way free reading makes teachers' lives easier is that it gives teachers a chance to relax and do some pleasure reading in the middle of their busy day. There is evidence, however, that doing other things that promote reading are pleasant and satisfying. Morrow (1985) reported on a 10-week study in which second-grade teachers were asked to read aloud to their students, tell and discuss stories, help children make their own books, use literature in the content areas, and establish comfortable and accessible library corners "containing at least five times as many books as there were children in the class" (p. 333). Before the program began, teachers were concerned that the increased use of literacy activities would take

☐ *Note 6 describes a study that shows promoting reading is pleasant and satisfying for teachers.*

needed time from other subjects and from "skill development," and that there was not enough space for library corners.

After the project was complete, however, Morrow reported that all the teachers decided to maintain the library corners and continue doing at least some of the literacy activities. This decision was based "on how much children and teachers enjoyed and used the activities, how the teachers viewed their educational value, and the expediency with which they could be carried out. . . . At the conclusion of the project, none of the participants saw time or space as a problem, as they had before the project began" (p. 335). In fact, teachers in the comparison group found out about the library corners and set them up in their classrooms.

References

Alexander, F. 1986. *California assessment program: Annual report*. Sacramento: California State Department of Education.

Allington, R. 1980. Poor readers don't get to read much in reading groups. *Language Arts* 57: 872–876.

Anderson, R., P. Wilson, and L. Fielding. 1988. Growth in reading and how children spend their time outside of school. *Reading Research Quarterly* 23: 285–303.

Applebee, A. 1978. Teaching high-achievement students: A survey of the winners of the 1977 NCTE Achievement Awards in writing. *Research in the Teaching of English* 1: 41–53.

———. 1984. Writing and reasoning. *Review of Educational Research* 54: 577–596.

Applebee, A., J. Langer, and I. Mullis. 1986. *The writing report card*. Princeton, N.J.: Educational Testing Service.

Applebee, A., J. Langer, I. Mullis, L. Jenkins, and M. Foertsch. 1990. *Learning to write in our nation's schools: Instruction and achievement in 1988 at grades 4, 8, and 12*. Princeton, N.J.: Educational Testing Service.

Appleby, B., and J. Conner. 1965. Well, what did you think of it? *English Journal* 54: 606–612.

Aranha, M. 1985. Sustained silent reading goes east. *Reading Teacher* 39: 214–217.

Arlin, M., and G. Roth. 1978. Pupils' use of time while reading comics and books. *American Educational Research Journal* 5: 201–216.

Arnold, L. 1964. Writer's cramp and eyestrain—are they paying off? *English Journal* 53: 10–15.

Aronow, M. 1961. A study of the effect of individualized reading on children's reading test scores. *Reading Teacher* 15: 86–91.

Bader, L., J. Veatch, and J. Eldridge. 1987. Trade books or basal readers? *Reading Improvement* 24: 62–67.

Bailyn, L. 1959. Mass media and children: A study of exposure habits and cognitive effects. *Psychological Monographs* 73: 201–216.

Beck, I., M. McKeown, and E. McCaslin. 1983. Vocabulary development: Not all contexts are created equal. *Elementary School Journal* 83: 177–181.

Beentjes, J., and T. Van der Voort. 1988. Television's impact on children's reading skills: A review of research. *Reading Research Quarterly* 23: 389–413.

Biber, D. 1986. Spoken and written textual dimensions in English. *Language* 62: 384–414.

Blakely, W. 1958. A study of seventh grade children's reading of comic books as related to certain other variables. *Journal of Genetic Psychology* 93: 291–301.

Blosser, B. 1988. Television, reading and oral language development: The case of the Hispanic child. *NABE Journal* 13: 21–42.

Bohnhorst, B., and S. Sellars. 1959. Individual reading instruction vs. basal textbook instruction: Some tentative explorations. *Elementary English* 36: 185–190, 202.

Brandenburg, G. 1919. Some possibly secondary factors in spelling ability. *School and Society* 9: 632–636.

Brink, W. 1939. Reading interests of high-school pupils. *School Review* 47: 613–621.

Brocka, B. 1979. Comic books: In case you haven't noticed, they've changed. *Media and Methods* 15: 30–32.

Brown, J., J. Cramond, and R. Wilde. 1974. Displacement effects of television and the child's functional orientation to media. In *Children's understanding of television*, ed. J. Bryant and D. Anderson. New York: Academic Press, pp. 1–33.

Burger, S. 1989. Content-based ESL in a sheltered psychology course: Input, output, and outcomes. *TESL Canada* 6: 45–59.

Busch, J. 1978. Television's effects on reading: A case study. *Phi Beta Kappan* 59: 668–671.

Campbell, C., D. Griswald, and F. H. Smith. 1988. Effects of tradebook covers (hardback or paperback) on individualized reading choices by elementary-age children. *Reading Improvement* 25: 166–178.

Campbell, D., and J. Stanley. 1966. *Experimental and quasi-experimental designs for research*. Chicago: Rand McNally.

Carlsen, G. R., and A. Sherrill. 1988. *Voices of readers: How we come to love books*. Urbana, Ill.: NCTE.

Carson, B. 1990. *Gifted hands*. Grand Rapids, Mich.: Zondervan Books.

Carter, C. 1988. Does your child love to read? *Parade Magazine,* April 3.

Chandler, G. 1973. Research on books and reading in society in the United Kingdom. *International Library Review* 5: 277–282.

Chomsky, N. 1965. *Aspects of the theory of syntax*. Cambridge, Mass.: MIT Press.

Cleary, F. 1939. Why children read. *Wilson Library Bulletin* 14: 119–126.

Coffin, T. 1948. Television's effects on leisure-time activities. *Journal of Applied Psychology* 32: 550–558.

Cohen, D. 1968. The effect of literature on vocabulary and reading achievement. *Elementary English* 45: 209–217.

Collins, C. 1980. Sustained silent reading periods: Effect of teachers' behaviors and students' achievements. *Elementary School Journal* 81: 109–114.

Cook, W. 1912. Shall we teach spelling by rule? *Journal of Educational Psychology* 3: 316–325.

Cornman, O. 1902. *Spelling in the elementary school*. Boston: Ginn.

Cummins, J. 1991. Interdependence of first- and second-language proficiency in bilingual children. In *Language processing in bilingual children*, ed. E. Bialystok. Cambridge, England: Cambridge University Press, pp. 70–89.

Curtiss, H., and E. Dolch. 1939. Do spelling books teach spelling? *Elementary School Journal* 39: 584–592.

Cyrog, F. 1962. Self-selection in reading: Report of a longitudinal study. In *Claremont reading conference: 26th yearbook,* ed. M. Douglas. Claremont, Calif.: Claremont Graduate School, pp. 106–113.

D'Anna, C., E. Zechmeister, and J. Hall. 1991. Toward a meaningful definition of vocabulary size. *Journal of Reading Behavior* 23: 109–122.

Davis, R., and J. Lucas. 1971. An experiment in individualizing reading procedures. *Reading Teacher* 24: 737–743, 747.

Degrotsky, D. 1981. Television viewing and reading achievement of seventh and eighth graders. ERIC Document No. ED 215 291.

Dorrell, L., and E. Carroll. 1981. Spider-Man at the library. *School Library Journal* 27: 17–19.

Dressel, P., J. Schmid, and G. Kincaid. 1952. The effects of writing frequency upon essay-type writing proficiency at the college level. *Journal of Educational Research* 46: 285–293.

Duggins, J. 1976. The elementary self-contained classroom. In *The new hooked on books,* D. Fader. New York: Berkley Books, pp. 181–190.

Dulay, H., and M. Burt. 1977. Remarks on creativity in second language acquisition. In *Viewpoints on English as a second language,* ed. M. Burt, H. Dulay, and M. Finnocchiaro. New York: Regents, pp. 95–126.

Dulay, H., M. Burt, and S. Krashen. 1982. *Language two.* New York: Oxford University Press.

Elbow, P. 1973. *Writing without teachers.* New York: Oxford University Press.

Eller, R., C. Pappas, and E. Brown. 1988. The lexical development of kindergartners: Learning from written context. *Journal of Reading Behavior* 20: 5–24.

Elley, W. 1984. Exploring the reading difficulties of second language learners in Fiji. In *Reading in a second language,* ed. J. C. Alderson and A. Urquart. New York: Longman, pp. 281–301.

———. 1989. Vocabulary acquisition from listening to stories. *Reading Research Quarterly* 24: 174–187.

———. 1991. Acquiring literacy in a second language: The effect of book-based programs. *Language Learning* 41: 375–411.

Elley, W., I. Barham, H. Lamb, and M. Wyllie. 1976. The role of grammar in a secondary school curriculum. *Research in the Teaching of English* 10: 5–21.

Elley, W., and F. Mangubhai. 1983. The impact of reading on second language learning. *Reading Research Quarterly* 19: 53–67.

El-Shabbaz, E. 1964. *The autobiography of Malcolm X.* New York: Ballantine Books.

Evans, H., and J. Towner. 1975. Sustained silent reading: Does it increase skills? *Reading Teacher* 29: 155–156.

Evans, P., and N. Gleadow. 1983. Literacy: A study of literacy performance and leisure activities in Victoria, B.C. *Reading Canada Lecture* 2: 3–16.

Fader, D. 1976. *The new hooked on books.* New York: Berkley Books.

Fasick, A. 1973. Television language and book language. *Elementary English* 50: 125–131.

Feitelson, D., B. Kita, and Z. Goldstein. 1986. Effects of listening to series stories on first graders' comprehension and use of language. *Research in the Teaching of English* 20: 339–356.

Finegan, E., and N. Besnier. 1989. *Language: Its structure and use.* New York: Harcourt Brace.

Foertsch, M. 1992. *Reading in and out of school.* Washington, D.C.: U.S. Department of Education.

Frebody, P., and R. Anderson. 1983. Effects on text comprehension of differing proportions and locations of difficult vocabulary. *Journal of Reading Behavior* 15: 19–39.

Gadberry, S. 1980. Effects of restricting first graders' TV-viewing on leisure time use, IQ change, and cognitive style. *Journal of Applied Developmental Psychology* 1: 45–57.

Gallo, D. 1968. Free reading and book reports—an informal survey of grade eleven. *Journal of Reading* 11: 532–538.

Ganguli, A. 1989. Integrating writing in developmental mathematics. *College Teaching* 37: 140–142.

Gaver, M. 1963. *Effectiveness of centralized library service in elementary schools.* New Brunswick, N.J.: Rutgers University Press.

Gilbert, L. 1934a. Effect of spelling on reading in the ninth grade. *School Review* 42: 197–204.

———. 1934b. Effect of reading on spelling in the secondary schools. *California Quarterly of Secondary Education* 9: 269–275.

———. 1935. Study of the effect of reading on spelling. *Journal of Educational Research* 28: 570–576.

Goodman, K. 1982. *Language and literacy: The selected writings of Kenneth S. Goodman.* 2 vols. Ed. F. Gollasch. London: Routledge.

Goodman, K., and Y. Goodman. 1982. Spelling ability of a self-taught reader. In *Language and literacy: The selected writings of Kenneth S. Goodman,* vol. 2, ed. F. Gollasch. London: Routledge, pp. 135–142.

Gordon, I., and C. Clark. 1961. An experiment in individualized reading. *Childhood Education* 38: 112–113.

Goulden, R., P. Nation, and J. Read. 1990. How large can a receptive vocabulary be? *Applied Linguistics* 11: 341–363.

Gradman, H., and E. Hanania. 1991. Language learning background factors and ESL proficiency. *Modern Language Journal* 75: 39–51.

Graves, M., G. Brunett, and W. Stater. 1982. The reading vocabularies of primary grade children from varying geographic and social backgrounds. In *New inquiries in reading research and instruction,* ed. J. Niles and L. Harris. Rochester, N.Y.: National Reading Conference, pp. 99–104.

Greaney, V. 1970. A comparison of individualized and basal reader approaches to reading instruction. *Irish Journal of Education* 1: 19–29.

———. 1980. Factors related to the amount and type of leisure time reading. *Reading Research Quarterly* 15: 337–357.

Greaney, V., and M. Clarke. 1973. A longitudinal study of the effects of two reading methods on leisure-time reading habits. In *Reading: What of the future?* ed. D. Moyle. London: United Kingdom Reading Association, pp. 107–114.

Greaney, V., and M. Hegarty. 1987. Correlations of leisure time reading. *Journal of Research in Reading* 10: 3–20.

Hafner, L., B. Palmer, and S. Tullos. 1986. The differential reading interests of good and poor readers in the ninth grade. *Reading Improvement* 23: 39–42.

Hagerty, P., E. Hiebert, and M. Owens. 1989. Students' comprehension, writing, and perceptions in two approaches to literacy instruction. In *Cognitive and social perspectives for literacy research and instruction: 38th yearbook of the National Reading Conference,* ed. S. McCormick and J. Zutell. Chicago: National Reading Conference, pp. 453–459.

Haggan, M. 1991. Spelling errors in native Arabic-speaking English majors: A comparison between remedial students and fourth year students. *System* 19: 45–61.

Hammill, D., S. Larson, and G. McNutt. 1977. The effect of spelling instruction: A preliminary study. *Elementary School Journal* 78: 67–72.

Harris, M. 1949. Beginning reading without readers. *Childhood Education* 26: 164–167.

Haugaard, K. 1973. Comic books: A conduit to culture? *Reading Teacher* 27: 54–55.

Healy, A. 1963. Changing children's attitudes toward reading. *Elementary English* 40: 255–257, 279.

Heisler, F. 1947. A comparison of comic book and non–comic book readers of the elementary school. *Journal of Educational Research* 40: 458–464.

Herman, P., R. Anderson, P. D. Pearson, and W. Nagy. 1987. Incidental acquisition of word meanings from expositions with varied text features. *Reading Research Quarterly* 22: 263–284.

Heyns, B. 1978. *Summer learning and the effects of schooling.* New York: Academic Press.

Hillocks, G., Jr. 1986. *Research on written composition: New directions for teaching.* ED 265552. Urbana, Ill.: ERIC.

Himmelweit, H., A. Oppenheim, and P. Vince. 1958. *Television and the child.* New York: Oxford University Press.

Holt, S., and F. O'Tuel. 1989. The effect of sustained silent reading and writing on achievement and attitudes of seventh and eighth grade students reading two years below grade level. *Reading Improvement* 26: 290–297.

Houle, R., and C. Montmarquette. 1984. An empirical analysis of loans by school libraries. *Alberta Journal of Educational Research* 30: 104–114.

Hoult, T. 1949. Comic books and juvenile delinquency. *Sociology and Social Research* 33: 279–284.

Hughes, J. 1966. The myth of the spelling list. *National Elementary Principal* 46: 53–54.

Hunting, R. 1967. Recent studies of writing frequency. *Research in the Teaching of English* 1: 29–40.

Husar, M. 1967. Reading and more reading. *Elementary English* 44: 378–385, 382.

Inge, M. 1985. *The American comic book.* Columbus: Ohio State University.

Ingham, J. 1981. *Books and reading development: The Bradford book flood experiment.* London: Heinemann Educational Books.

Jacoby, L., and A. Hollingshead. 1990. Reading student essays may be hazardous to your spelling: Effects of reading incorrectly and correctly spelled words. *Canadian Journal of Psychology* 44: 345–358.

Janopoulos, M. 1986. The relationship of pleasure reading and second language writing proficiency. *TESOL Quarterly* 20: 763–768.

Jenkins, M. 1957. Self-selection in reading. *Reading Teacher* 10: 84–90.

Johnson, R. 1965. Individualized and basal primary reading programs. *Reading Teacher* 42: 902–904, 915.

Kaplan, J., and E. Palhinda. 1981. Non-native speakers of English and their composition abilities: A review and analysis. In *Linguistics and literacy,* ed. W. Frawley. New York: Plenum Press, pp. 425–457.

Klesius, J., P. Griffith, and P. Zielonka. 1991. A whole language and traditional instruction comparison: Overall effectiveness and development of the alphabetic principle. *Reading Research and Instruction* 30: 47–61.

Konopak, B. 1988. Effects of inconsiderate vs. considerate text on secondary students' vocabulary learning. *Journal of Reading Behavior* 20: 25–41.

Krashen, S. 1978. On the acquisition of planned discourse: Written English as a second dialect. In *Claremont reading conference: 42nd yearbook,* ed. M. Douglas. Claremont, Calif.: Claremont Graduate School, pp. 173–185.

———. 1982. *Principles and practice in second language acquisition.* New York: Prentice Hall.

———. 1984. *Writing: Research, theory, and applications.* Torrance, Calif.: Laredo Publishing.

———. 1985a. *Inquiries and insights.* Menlo Park, Calif.: Alemany Press.

———. 1985b. *The input hypothesis: Issues and implications.* Torrance, Calif.: Laredo Publishing.

———. 1988. Do we learn to read by reading? The relationship between free reading and reading ability. In *Linguistics in context: Connecting observation and understanding,* ed. D. Tannen. Norwood, N.J.: Ablex, pp. 269–298.

———. 1989. We acquire vocabulary and spelling by reading: Additional evidence for the Input Hypothesis. *Modern Language Journal* 73: 440–464.

———. 1990. How reading and writing make you smarter, or, how smart people read and write. In *Linguistics, language teaching, and language acquisition,* ed. J. Alatis. Georgetown University Round Table on Languages and Linguistics, Washington, D.C.: Georgetown University, pp. 364–376.

Krashen, S., and D. Biber. 1988. *On course: Bilingual education's success in California.* Sacramento: California Association for Bilingual Education.

Krashen, S., and H. White. 1991. Is spelling acquired or learned? A re-analysis of Rice (1897) and Cornman (1902). *ITL: Review of Applied Linguistics* 91–92: 1–48.

Kyte, G. 1948. When spelling has been mastered in the elementary school. *Journal of Educational Research* 42: 47–53.

LaBrant, L. 1958. An evaluation of free reading. In *Research in the three R's*, ed. C. Hunnicutt and W. Iverson. New York: Harper and Brothers, pp. 154–161.

Lamme, L. 1976. Are reading habits and abilities related? *Reading Teacher* 30: 21–27.

Lancaster, T. 1928. A study of the voluntary reading of pupils in grades IV–VIII. *Elementary School Journal* 28: 525–537.

Langer, J., and A. Applebee. 1987. *How writing shapes thinking*. Urbana, Ill.: National Council of Teachers of English.

Lawson, H. 1968. Effects of free reading on the reading achievement of sixth grade pupils. In *Forging ahead in reading*, ed. J. A. Figurel. Newark, Del.: International Reading Association, pp. 501–504.

Leung, C., and J. Pikulski. 1990. Incidental learning of word meanings by kindergarten and first grade children through repeated read aloud events. In *Literacy theory and research: Analysis from multiple paradigms*, ed. J. Zutell and S. McCormick. Chicago: National Reading Conference, pp. 231–240.

Liberman, M. 1979. The verbal language of television. *Journal of Reading* 26: 602–609.

Lokke, V., and G. Wykoff. 1948. "Double writing" in freshman composition—an experiment. *School and Society* 68: 437–439.

Lomax, C. 1976. Interest in books and stories at nursery school. *Educational Research* 19: 110–112.

Lorge, I., and J. Chall. 1963. Estimating the size of vocabularies of children and adults: An analysis of methodological issues. *Journal of Experimental Education* 32: 147–157.

Lowrey, L., and W. Grafft. 1965. Paperback books and reading attitudes. *Reading Teacher* 21: 618–623.

Maccoby, E. 1951. Television: Its impact on school children. *Public Opinion Quarterly* 15: 421–444.

Manning, G., and M. Manning. 1984. What models of recreational reading make a difference? *Reading World* May: 375–380.

Marshall, J. 1987. The effects of writing on students' understanding of literary texts. *Research in the Teaching of English* 21: 30–63.

Mathabane, M. 1986. *Kaffir boy.* New York: Plume.

Maynes, F. 1981. Uninterrupted sustained silent reading. *Reading Research Quarterly* 17: 159–160.

McCracken, R., and M. McCracken. 1978. Modeling is the key to sustained silent reading. *Reading Teacher* 31: 406–408.

McDonald, J., T. Harris, and J. Mann. 1966. Individual versus group instruction in first grade reading. *Reading Teacher* 19: 643–646, 652.

McEvoy, G., and C. Vincent. 1980. Who reads and why? *Journal of Communication* 30: 134–140.

McKenna, M., D. Kear, and R. Ellsworth. 1991. Developmental trends in children's use of print media: A national study. In *Learner factors/teacher factors: Issues in literacy research and instruction,* ed. J. Zutell and S. McCormick. Chicago: National Reading Conference, pp. 319–324.

Miller, G. 1977. *Spontaneous apprentices: Children and language.* New York: Seabury.

Monteith, M. 1980. How well does the average American read? Some facts, figures and opinions. *Journal of Reading* 20: 460–464.

Morrow, L. 1982. Relationships between literature programs, library corner designs, and children's use of literature. *Journal of Educational Research* 75: 339–344.

———. 1983. Home and school correlates of early interest in literature. *Journal of Educational Research* 76: 221–230.

———. 1985. Field-based research on voluntary reading: A process for teachers' learning and change. *Reading Teacher* 39: 331–337.

Morrow, L., and C. Weinstein. 1982. Increasing children's use of literature through program and physical changes. *Elementary School Journal* 83: 131–137.

————. 1986. Encouraging voluntary reading: The impact of a literature program on children's use of library centers. *Reading Research Quarterly* 21: 330–346.

Murray, J., and S. Kippax. 1978. Children's social behavior in three towns with differing television experience. *Reading Teacher* 28: 19–29.

Nagy, W., R. Anderson, and P. Herman. 1987. Learning word meanings from context during normal reading. *American Educational Research Journal* 24: 237–270.

Nagy, W., and P. Herman. 1987. Breadth and depth of vocabulary knowledge: Implications for acquisition and instruction. In *The nature of vocabulary acquisition*, ed. M. McKeown and M. Curtiss. Hillsdale, N.J.: Erlbaum, pp. 19–35.

Nagy, W., P. Herman, and R. Anderson. 1985. Learning words from context. *Reading Research Quarterly* 20: 233–253.

Nell, V. 1988. The psychology of reading for pleasure: Needs and gratifications. *Reading Research Quarterly* 23: 6–50.

Neuman, S. 1986. The home environment and fifth-grade students' leisure reading. *Elementary School Journal* 86: 335–343.

————. 1988. The displacement effect: Assessing the relation between television viewing and reading performance. *Reading Research Quarterly* 23: 414–440.

Newell, G. 1984. Learning while writing in two content areas: A case study/protocol analysis. *Research in the Teaching of English* 18: 265–287.

Newell, G., and P. Winograd. 1989. The effects of writing on learning from expository text. *Written Communication* 6: 196–217.

Nisbet, S. 1941. The scientific investigation of spelling instruction: Two preliminary problems. *British Journal of Educational Psychology* 11: 150.

O'Brian, I. 1931. A comparison of the use of intensive training and wide reading in the improvement of reading. *Educational Method* 10: 346–349.

Oliver, M. 1973. The effect of high intensity practice on reading comprehension. *Reading Improvement* 10: 16–18.

———. 1976. The effect of high intensity practice on reading achievement. *Reading Improvement* 13: 226–228.

Ormrod, J. 1986. Learning to spell while reading: A follow-up study. *Perceptual and Motor Skills* 63: 652–654.

Parrish, B. 1983. Put a little romantic fiction into your reading program. *Journal of Reading* 26: 610–615.

Parrish, B., and K. Atwood. 1985. Enticing readers: The teen romance craze. *California Reader* 18: 22–27.

Pfau, D. 1967. Effects of planned recreational reading programs. *Reading Teacher* 21: 34–39.

Pitts, M., H. White, and S. Krashen. 1989. Acquiring second language vocabulary through reading: A replication of the Clockwork Orange study using second language acquirers. *Reading in a Foreign Language* 5: 271–275.

Pitts, S. 1986. Read aloud to adult learners? Of course! *Reading Psychology: An International Quarterly* 7: 35–42.

Polak, J., and S. Krashen. 1988. Do we need to teach spelling? The relationship between spelling and voluntary reading among community college ESL students. *TESOL Quarterly* 22: 141–146.

Postman, N. 1983. The disappearing child. *Educational Leadership* 40: 10–17.

Potter, W. 1987. Does television viewing hinder academic achievement among adolescents? *Human Communications Research* 14: 27–46.

Reed, C. 1985. *Reading adolescents: The young adult book and the school.* New York: Holt Rinehart Winston.

Rehder, L. 1980. Reading skills in a paperback classroom. *Reading Horizons* 21: 16–21.

Rice, E. 1986. The everyday activities of adults: Implications for prose recall–Part I. *Educational Gerontology* 12: 173–186.

Rice, J. 1897. The futility of the spelling grind. *Forum* 23: 163–172, 409–419.

Richards, A. 1920. Spelling and the individual system. *School and Society* 10: 647–650.

Robinson, J. 1972. Television's impact on everyday life: Some cross-national evidence. In *Television and Social Behavior,* vol. 4, ed. E. Rubinstein, G. Comstock, and J. Murray. Rockwell, Md.: National Institute of Mental Health, pp. 410–431.

———. 1980. The changing reading habits of the American public. *Journal of Communication* 30: 141–152.

Ross, P. 1978. Getting books into those empty hands. *Reading Teacher* 31: 397–399.

Rucker, B. 1982. Magazines and teenage reading skills: Two controlled field experiments. *Journalism Quarterly* 59: 28–33.

Salyer, M. 1987. A comparison of the learning characteristics of good and poor ESL writers. *Applied Linguistics Interest Section Newsletter, TESOL,* 8: 2–3.

San Diego County. 1965. A plan for research. In *Individualized reading: Readings,* ed. S. Duker. Metuchen, N.J.: Scarecrow Press, pp. 359–363.

Saragi, Y., P. Nation, and G. Meister. 1978. Vocabulary learning and reading. *System* 6: 70–78.

Sartain, H. 1960. The Roseville experiment with individualized reading. *Reading Teacher* 12: 277–281.

Schatz, E., and R. S. Baldwin. 1986. Context clues are unreliable predictors of word meanings. *Reading Research Quarterly* 20: 439–453.

Schon, I., K. Hopkins, and C. Vojir. 1984. The effects of Spanish reading emphasis on the English and Spanish reading abilities of Hispanic high school students. *Bilingual Review* 11: 33–39.

———. 1985. The effects of special reading time in Spanish on the reading abilities and attitudes of Hispanic junior high school students. *Journal of Psycholinguistics Research* 14: 57–65.

Schoolboys of Barbiana. 1970. *Letter to a teacher.* New York: Vintage Books.

Schoonover, R. 1938. The case for voluminous reading. *English Journal* 27: 114–118.

Schramm, W., J. Lyle, and E. Parker. 1961. *Television in the lives of our children.* Stanford, Calif.: Stanford University Press.

References

Schwartzenberg, H. 1962. What children think of individualized reading. *Reading Teacher* 16: 86–89.

Seashore, R., and L. Eckerson. 1940. The measurement of individual differences in general English vocabularies. *Journal of Educational Psychology* 31: 14–31.

Shooter, J. 1986. Marvel and me. In *The comic book price guide,* ed. R. Overstreet. New York: Harmony Books, A85–96.

Slover, V. 1959. Comic books vs. story books. *Elementary English* 36: 319–322.

Smith, F. 1982a. *Writing and the writer.* New York: Holt Rinehart Winston.

———. 1983. Reading like a writer. *Language Arts* 60: 558–567. Reprinted in F. Smith. *Joining the literacy club.* Portsmouth, N.H.: Heinemann, 1988.

———. 1988a. *Understanding reading.* Hillsdale, N.J.: Erlbaum.

———. 1988b. *Joining the literacy club.* Portsmouth, N.H.: Heinemann.

Smith, M. 1941. Measurement of the size of general English vocabulary through the elementary grades and high school. *Genetic Psychology Monographs* 24: 311–345.

Smith, R., and G. Supanich. 1984. *The vocabulary scores of company presidents.* Chicago: Johnson O'Connor Research Foundation Technical Report 1984–1.

Snow, C., W. Barnes, J. Chandler, I. Goodman, and H. Hemphill. 1991. *Unfulfilled expectations: Home and school influences on literacy.* Cambridge, Mass.: Harvard University Press.

Sommers, N. 1980. Revision strategies of student writers and experienced adult writers. *College Composition and Communication* 31: 378–388.

Southgate, V., H. Arnold, and S. Johnson. 1981. *Extending beginning reading.* London: Heinemann Educational Books.

Sperzl, E. 1948. The effect of comic books on vocabulary growth and reading comprehension. *Elementary English* 25: 109–113.

Stahl, S., M. Richek, and R. Vandevier. 1991. Learning meaning vocabulary through listening: A sixth-grade replication. In *Learner factors/teacher factors: Issues in literacy research and instruction,* ed. J. Zutell and S. McCormick. Chicago: National Reading Conference, pp. 185–192.

Stanovich, K., and R. West. 1989. Exposure to print and orthographic process-ing. *Reading Research Quarterly* 24: 402–433.

Stedman, L., and C. Kaestle. 1987. Literacy and reading performance in the United States, from 1880 to the present. *Reading Research Quarterly* 22: 59–78.

Summers, E., and J. V. McClelland. 1982. A field-based evaluation of sustained silent reading (SSR) in intermediate grades. *Alberta Journal of Educational Research* 28: 110–112.

Sutton, R. 1985. Librarians and the paperback romance. *School Library Journal* 32: 25–29.

Swain, E. 1978. Using comic books to teach reading and language arts. *Journal of Reading* 22: 253–258.

Swanton, S. 1984. Minds alive: What and why gifted students read for pleasure. *School Library Journal* 30: 99–102.

Thompson, R. 1930. *The effectiveness of modern spelling instruction.* New York: Columbia University Teacher's College (Contributions to Education, No. 436).

Thorndike, R. 1941. Words and the comics. *Journal of Experimental Education* 10: 110–113.

———. 1973. *Reading comprehension education in fifteen countries.* New York: Halsted Press.

Trelease, J. 1982. *The read-aloud handbook.* New York: Penguin.

Twadell, F. 1973. Vocabulary expansion in the TESOL classroom. *TESOL Quar-terly* 7: 61–78.

Varble, M. 1990. Analysis of writing samples of students taught by teachers using whole language and traditional approaches. *Journal of Educational Research* 83: 245–251.

Wayne, R. 1954. Survey of interest in comic books. *School Activities* 25: 244.

Wendelin, K., and R. A. Zinck. 1983. How students make book choices. *Reading Horizons* 23: 84–88.

Wertham, F. 1954. *Seduction of the innocent.* New York: Rinehart.

References

White, T., M. Graves, and W. Slater. 1990. Growth of reading vocabulary in diverse elementary schools: Decoding and word meaning. *Journal of Educational Psychology* 82: 281–290.

Wilde, S. 1990. A proposal for a new spelling curriculum. *Elementary School Journal* 90: 275–290.

Williams, P., E. Haertel, G. Haertel, and H. Walberg. 1982. The impact of leisure-time television on school learning: A research synthesis. *American Educational Research Journal* 19: 19–50.

Willig, A. 1985. A meta-analysis of selected studies on the effectiveness of bilingual education. *Review of Educational Research* 55: 269–317.

Witty, P. 1941. Reading the comics: A comparative study. *Journal of Experimental Education* 10: 105–109.

Witty, P., and R. Sizemore. 1954. Reading the comics: A summary of studies and an evaluation, I. *Elementary English* 31: 501–506.

———. 1955. Reading the comics: A summary of studies and an evaluation, III. *Elementary English* 32: 109–114.

Wolf, A., and L. Mikulecky. 1978. Effects of uninterrupted sustained silent reading and of reading skills instruction on changes in secondary school students' reading attitudes and achievement. *27th Yearbook of the National Reading Conference.* National Reading Conference, Clemson, S.C., pp. 226–228.

Wollner, M. 1949. *Children's voluntary reading as an expression of individuality.* New York: Columbia University Teacher's College.

Wright, G. 1979. The comic book: A forgotten medium in the classroom. *Reading Teacher* 33: 158–161.

Wright, R. 1966. *Black boy.* New York: Harper and Row.

Zuckerman, D., D. Singer, and J. Singer. 1980. Television viewing, children's reading, and related classroom behavior. *Journal of Communication* 32: 166–174.

Researcher Index

Alexander, F., 73, 91
Allington, R., 24, 91
Anderson, R., 5, 8, 9, 11, 14, 15, 19, 28, 51, 55, 67, 91, 95, 97, 102
Applebee, A., 6, 73, 74, 77, 78, 91, 100
Appleby, B., 45, 91
Aranha, M., 26, 91
Arlin, M., 55, 67, 91
Arnold, H., 38, 64, 65, 105
Arnold, L., 75, 91
Aronow, M., 27, 92
Atwood, K., 9, 61, 62, 103

Bader, L., 26, 65, 92
Bailyn, L., 56, 66, 92
Baldwin, R. S., 28, 104
Barham, I., 22, 95
Barnes, W., 20, 35, 36, 74, 105
Beck, I., 9, 92
Beentjes, J., 80, 82, 83, 92
Besnier, N., 14, 30, 95
Biber, D., 68, 88, 92, 99
Blakely, W., 48, 55, 56, 92
Blosser, B., 82, 92
Bohnhorst, B., 27, 92
Brandenburg, G., 20, 92
Brink, W., 6, 92
Brocka, B., 79, 92
Brown, E., 40, 94
Brown, J., 79, 92
Brunett, G., 32, 96
Burger, S., 75, 93
Burt, M., 70, 94
Busch, J., 80, 93

Campbell, C., 46, 80, 93
Campbell, D., 28, 93
Carlsen, G. R., 41–42, 44, 79, 86, 93
Carroll, E., 56–57, 94
Chall, J., 14, 30, 100
Chandler, G., 38, 93
Chandler, J., 20, 35, 36, 74, 105
Chomsky, N., 71, 93
Clark, C., 26, 96
Clarke, M., 40, 97
Cleary, F., 34, 38, 87, 93
Coffin, T., 79, 93
Cohen, D., 40, 93
Collins, C., 26, 93
Conner, J., 45, 91
Cook, W., 20–21, 31, 93
Cornman, O., 18, 31, 93
Cramond, J., 79, 92
Cummins, J., 88, 93
Curtiss, H., 19, 94
Cyrog, F., 27, 94

D'Anna, C., 30, 94
Davis, R., 26, 94
Degrotsky, D., 83, 94
Dichara (cited in Krashen 1978), 6
Dolch, E., 19, 94
Dorrell, L., 56–57, 94
Dressel, P., 75, 94
Duggins, J., 46, 94
Dulay, H., 70, 94

Eckerson, L., 14, 105
Elbow, P., 76, 94

Subject Index

Weaver, Dennis, ix
Winfrey, Oprah, ix,
Word choice (in writing), 6
Wright, Richard, 16–17
Writing
    to communicate, 76
    frequency of, 74
    learning to write by, 73–75
    to think, 76
    and thinking, 72

Writing ability, 3, 6, 71–78
Writing studies by level
    adult, 74
    college, 75, 78
    elementary, 74
    secondary, 74, 77–78
Writing style, 5, 23, 68, 72–78
    and problem solving, 72
    a product of reading, 75–76, 84